P9-BBU-087

PRAISE FOR *MAKE IT HAPPEN*

"Want to exchange your fear for faith and move forward into all God has for you? Lara shows by example how to sort through the clutter and chaos of your life to find what really matters. So many of us hold dreams and we don't know what to do with them. Lara is a master at unraveling purpose and helping you move forward with freedom and joy."

—JENNIE ALLEN
FOUNDER, IF:GATHERING AND AUTHOR, *RESTLESS*

"Finally there's someone to remind us that making things happen is more than just trying to accomplish everything that might happen on our to-do lists. Instead she explains how we often glorify busyness and then goes on to offer important helps to find and follow the real success equation—the one that will allow you to live on purpose."

—JEREMY COWART
ARTIST, AUTHOR, HUMANITARIAN

"My days and weeks are filled with meeting with women of our generation, online and in my living room. I can't tell you how often I find myself asking them, 'Have you heard of Lara Casey?' God has wired Lara in the most beautiful way to fire women up while simultaneously soaking them in grace and hope through her story and her wisdom. This book is one that I cannot wait to pass across the table because I know it offers the truth and encouragement that so many women are desperately searching for."

—JESS CONNOLLY
ENTREPRENEUR AND WRITER

"If you've spent most of your life living between feeling like you are either not enough or way too much, you will want to read *Make It Happen*. Lara Casey's personal history and her relentless pursuit of perfection (and ultimate surrender to grace) provide the perfect backdrop to help you go from feeling overwhelmed to living on purpose. You won't put down the book feeling more overwhelmed, but with an actionable plan filled with reminders from Lara that you're already enough and never too much."

—HAYLEY MORGAN
COFOUNDER, INFLUENCE NETWORK
CREATIVE DIRECTOR, WILDLY CO.

MAKE IT HAPPEN

MAKE IT HAPPEN

SURRENDER YOUR FEAR
Take the Leap
LIVE ON PURPOSE

LARA CASEY

W PUBLISHING GROUP

AN IMPRINT OF THOMAS NELSON

© 2014 Lara Casey

All rights reserved. No portion of this book may be reproduced, stored in a retrieval system, or transmitted in any form or by any means—electronic, mechanical, photocopy, recording, scanning, or other—except for brief quotations in critical reviews or articles, without the prior written permission of the publisher.

Published in Nashville, Tennessee, by W Publishing Group, an imprint of Thomas Nelson.

Thomas Nelson titles may be purchased in bulk for educational, business, fund-raising, or sales promotional use. For information, please e-mail SpecialMarkets@ ThomasNelson.com.

Unless otherwise marked, Scripture quotations are taken from the Holy Bible, New International Version®, NIV®. Copyright © 1973, 1978, 1984, 2011 by Biblica, Inc.™ Used by permission of Zondervan. All rights reserved worldwide. www.zondervan.com

Scripture quotations marked ESV are taken from the English Standard Version. © 2001 by Crossway Bibles, a division of Good News Publishers.

Scripture quotations marked MSG are taken from *The Message* by Eugene H. Peterson. © 1993, 1994, 1995, 1996, 2000. Used by permission of NavPress Publishing Group. All rights reserved.

Scripture quotations marked NLT are taken from the *Holy Bible*, New Living Translation, copyright © 1996, 2004, 2007 by Tyndale House Foundation. Used by permission of Tyndale House Publishers, Inc., Carol Stream, IL 60188. All rights reserved.

ISBN 978-0-529-10150-1

Library of Congress Cataloging-in-Publication Data

Casey, Lara.
  Make it happen : surrender your fear. take the leap. live on purpose / Lara Casey.
     pages cm
  Includes bibliographical references.
  ISBN 978-0-529-10150-1 (trade paper)
  1. Self-actualization (Psychology)—Religious aspects—Christianity. 2. Fear—Religious aspects—Christianity. 3. Courage. 4. Christian life. I. Title.
  BV4598.2.C38 2014
  248.4—dc23   2014022260

Printed in the United States of America

16 17 18 RRD 12 11 10 9 8

Me: Gracie, what should I write here?
Grace: Mommeee, yooo shud wite "I lub you!"
Me: That's a great idea, sweet pea! I love you, Grace.

May you know how DEEP and WIDE
His love is for you.

CONTENTS

CONTENTS

ACKNOWLEDGMENTS

This book comes from the thousands of stories shared with me over the years from women who want to make what matters happen. To those who have shared their lives with me online, in workshops, and in long conversations over sweet tea on my porch—thank you.

The women I work with each day at *Southern Weddings*—Emily Thomas, Lisa Olson, Marissa Kloess, Kristin Winchester, Nicole Yang—not only ran our company while I was writing this book, but they encouraged me daily. Ladies, you are the bee's knees. This book came from your hearts as much as it did from mine.

My very first Bible, which was given to me by my grandfather, was a King James Version, published by Thomas Nelson. When God put it on my heart to write this book, I prayed, "God, if it's Your will, I would love to write a book with Thomas Nelson." God heard my prayer and not only allowed me to write these pages to you, but He brought incredible people alongside me to make it happen. Debbie Wickwire, thank you for guiding me with such heart, helping me laugh, heal, and trust that God sat me down at this keyboard for a reason. Your encouragement shaped each word. Katie Bond, Stephanie Newton, Matt Baugher, Emily Sweeney, Paula Major, Carol Martin, Caroline Green, Kristi Smith, Meaghan Porter, Adria Haley, Andrea Lucado, Belinda Bass, Julie Allen, Jennifer Stair, and the Thomas Nelson team, thank you for giving me this chance to share what He has done in my life.

Enormous thanks to Seth Fishman, who introduced me to my agent, Claudia Cross, at Folio Literary. Claudia, the first time I spoke with you, I felt the same way I did in starting a magazine—I had no idea what I was doing! But you put me at ease immediately. I am so grateful.

Many dear friends have walked with me on this journey, reminding me I am not alone and encouraging me in the (many) times when I felt like I'd never ever finish: Emily Ley, Gina Zeidler, Natalie and Richie Norton, Nancy and Will Ray, Karen Stott, Rhiannon Bosse, Hannah Brencher, Carrie McQuaid, Kate Dunlap, Jessi Connoly, Hayley Morgan, Amber Housley, Emily Hansel, Jessie Bell, Tijuana Goodwin, Whitney Afonso, my sister Kathy, the Making Things Happen community, and so many more—thank you.

Mom, thank you for nurturing our family like you do your garden, with fierce love and devotion. Dad, thanks for always reminding me that my creative gifts matter. Your faith and zest for life inspire me.

Michael and Suzy, your encouragement through this book process helped me to let go of perfection and focus on purpose.

Mitch and Jan, Phil and Leslie, Bob and Buena, Ted and Sonya, and our local church family, your bear hugs changed *everything*.

ACKNOWLEDGMENTS

Meredith Blankenship and Susan Wooden, it's because you love my daughter, Grace, that I was able to write these words. I know God is good because He gave me you.

Gracie, you can't read words yet, but you can read hearts. I'll give you my thanks with ten thousand hugs, boo-boo kisses, and silly dances in the kitchen over the next however-many years God lets me. When you are able to read this, know that your boundless love and joy filled me every single day I wrote. You are my sunshine.

Ari, thank you for helping me unearth these words and for drying my tears as I wrote about our hardest times. You helped turn those tears into a deeper joy. This book is my love song to God in thanks for you.

Grandpa, thank you for giving me that first Bible.

WELCOME TO YOUR START

today is the DAY that EVERYTHING changes.

I can do this. *It's my body. I can make this happen.*

I tried to control the pain, but the more I fought, the more overwhelming it became. The tension came in waves with short releases between—not enough time to renew my strength, but enough time to doubt my ability to get through. Doubt turned to desperation. *Why am I so weak? I can't do this!*

I pleaded for a way out. Then another wave of pain hit, more intense than the last. I knew my life would completely change if I let go. And I was afraid of change, afraid of more pain, afraid not to be in control, afraid to trust in the unknown.

Exhausted from the battle against the inevitable, I realized there was no way out but through. I couldn't run from the pain or restrain it any longer. It had to come. It was part of the plan. So I took the leap and let go.

The day of Grace's birth was the day I learned a life-altering truth: my need for control was holding life back. New life would come not by my own might but through surrender.

In the same way, we all must let go of where we are in order for new life to come. We must die a little. Sometimes a lot. Making it happen—a life lived on purpose—comes by surrendering control.

But how in the world does surrendering help us realize big dreams? How does letting go help us *do* stuff?

Maybe you are in a dead-end job or a lifeless marriage. Maybe you are at the starting line with talent and passion, but you have no idea how to use them to make a life. Maybe the laundry keeps piling up, and your little one just won't stop crying, and you hardly have time to pee. Maybe your money and time feel beyond your control. Maybe you are lost and alone, and you sometimes feel like you might crack.

And maybe, without realizing it, you are exactly where you are supposed to be in order to take a leap of faith.

TAKE A DEEP BREATH

Imagine I'm sitting right in front of you, looking into your eyes. Hi.

Now take a deep breath. I think I know how you feel right now. You are overwhelmed, worried, or stressed—or all three squared. Either you know what you want and don't know how to make it happen, or you feel like you might explode trying to figure it all out. You're just not *sure*, and you want to be sure more than anything.

You want to make big things happen in your life, but you don't have time, patience, money, sleep, rest, or peace. You're burning the candle at both ends and in the middle. You feel pressured to keep going, be better, move faster, do more, and be perfect. You feel as though you'll never get there. In fact, you're not even sure where *there* is anymore.

You're often paralyzed by fear. Instead of taking action on the things that keep pulling at your heart, you get out your phone and look at what other people are doing. You may be considering doing that right this second because reading this is mildly uncomfortable. But stay with me here.

Perhaps someone once told you that you weren't enough—and you started to believe it. But now you're feeling restless. You know there is something bigger than the life you are currently living.

You skipped the deep-breath part a few paragraphs back, didn't you? Oh, friend. If it were possible for me to jump through the page and hug you, I would do that right now. I was there just a few short years ago. I spent most of my life stuck in the cement shoes of fear. I had become a burned-out workaholic buried by debt, depression, and a failing marriage.

I realized I had no idea who I really was. I would often ask myself these questions:

- *Who am I?*
- *What is my purpose?*
- *What am I supposed to be going after in life?*
- *I want to make it happen, but what is "it"?*

Have you been asking yourself those same questions?

Are you feeling restless right now? Do you feel there's something bigger than the life you're living?

USE WHAT YOU HAVE RIGHT NOW

This book is your invitation to stop striving, be still, and let go of your struggles and fear. To surrender what *feels* like everything, to gain what really *is* everything. You were created to do more than what can possibly be held in your tiny world all by your lonesome.

You were created for a purpose. You were created to shine.

It's time to be free.

Free of shame.

Free of fear.

Free to fully live.

Friend, you don't need to be ready or perfect to make what matters happen. A life of purpose—living for something bigger than yourself—is not about achieving your dream job or the ideal circumstances or the perfect timing. Use what you have, where you are, right now, *on purpose.*

HOW TO USE THIS BOOK

This is not a reading-only book. I'm going to ask you to *do* stuff, because just sitting with your thoughts hasn't been getting you anywhere. So let's shake things up together.

In parts 1 through 3, I'll share some of my personal story as a springboard to inspire and equip you to take intentional action. As you read chapters 1 through 12, I encourage you to interact with my story by journaling or talking out your thoughts as you read. Respond and personalize the truths you uncover by working through the application sidebars included in each chapter. Then begin to live out the life lessons as you "Take Action" in the section provided at the end of each chapter.

The final section of the book, "Your Guide to Make It Happen," is a special workbook-style action guide created just for you. This section details five practical, doable action steps you can apply—starting right now—to step into the life for which you are longing.

Please note: there's no perfect way to read this book. If you see a chapter title that intrigues you, start there. Or if you want to skip ahead to "Your Guide to Make It Happen," that's okay. This book is *your* tool to make things happen and leap into a life of purpose.

What are you waiting for? What has been holding you back from fully living? Write it below.

_____

_____

_____

_____

Now draw a line through it to symbolize the fresh start you are making by reading this book.

DON'T WAIT TO LIVE

As you go through these pages, don't wait to take action. Don't wait for *me* to say go! Don't wait for the right words or the best plan or the perfect time. Just start where you are. Read the stories, work through the sidebars, do the action steps, make it happen!

The enemy of taking action is the false belief in "someday." Do the good you know you ought to do—and start now. Do it knowing that you might not have as much time as you think. The alternative is to do nothing, and that does, well, nothing. *Don't wait to live.*

This is the story of how I faced my fear, took the leap, and got a life. In my case, I got a perfectly imperfect, fulfilling, joyful life as a mama, a working woman, and a grateful wife. This is the story of how I chose to make "it" happen and how you can too. "It" is what matters. "It" is what lasts longer than you. "It" is a greater purpose than ours.

The time has come—*your* time has come—to take a leap of faith and live a life of purpose.

Welcome to your start.

P.S. I know you want answers, clarity, and a plan yesterday. Know that the best things in life come little by little. A truth to carry with you as you do the work ahead: "There are no shortcuts to any place worth going" (Beverly Sills).

P.P.S. I know "P.S." is meant for letters, but making it happen also means breaking the rules.

PART ONE

Surrender Your Fear

1

STOP CHASING PERFECT

Choose PURPOSE over PERFECT.

When asked what they are proudest of in life, many people describe honors or awards. My Grandpa Cecil would simply pull out a picture of his wife. They met in rural Alabama. Celeste Virginia—a fiery redhead—was the youngest daughter in a large Southern family of eleven, but she was ahead of her time; she earned a living as a traveling theater director. Cecil, one of eight children himself, signed up to be an extra in one of her plays with his brothers. It was love at first sight. But Celeste had to travel with the show, and Cecil was drafted into the army. They wrote epic love letters for two years before finally tying the knot in a tiny ceremony at her family home. Grandpa loved three things most, in this order: the Bible, his bride, and his vegetable garden. Well, and cheating at checkers, but that's another story.

Grandpa tended to his sweet tomato plants just as he tended to Grandma Celeste—with love. He loved his Early Girls so much that when my mom was in college, he would carefully wrap a handpicked selection in a newspaper-padded box and mail it to her to enjoy.

I have a vivid memory of being in the community garden with him as he watered his crops in his later years. Grandpa would sink his hands into damp, mineral-drenched soil and tell me what heaven was going to be like. Grandpa's life was like a beautiful creek, flowing with fresh water and trickling with a soothing sound that made everything all right. My life, on the other hand, was more like an avalanche: frozen water crashing down a mountain at breakneck speed.

I wanted the glamorous life I saw in movies: travel, adventure, and sweeping love. My focus in high school was theater, boys, and making my parents proud.

I loved the smell of sawdust from building sets, and most of all I loved the applause. When we saw the audience rise for a standing ovation, it felt like we were a part of something bigger. We were making people *feel* something. I relished the stage for its sense of wonder. Even at that young age, I knew art was important. Thanks to my parents, I knew my creative gifts mattered. So I lived and breathed painting, design, music, and theater.

During a high school English class, my proud mama swept into the classroom holding a Carnegie Mellon T-shirt and my acceptance letter. I was one of sixteen students chosen that year for their music theater program. I might have burst out in song.

At our convocation ceremony, we were told to look to our left and to our right: "One of you won't be standing here at graduation. If you can get through four years at CMU, you will be able to get through anything." I laughed naively and dove in to fifty hours a week of dance, acting, voice, movement, speech, and music.

Five days a week, for hours, I scrutinized myself in the mirror as I would plié and relevé my heart out. I was terrible at ballet. Turns out, I was terrible at a lot of things. Suddenly I wasn't the best anymore. I was used to my parents telling me everything I did was great. I was used to getting every role I wanted in high school and being met with standing ovations. Then I got to college, and people started saying, "Work harder."

I refused to settle for mediocrity, so I tried to be the best in every area: performance, popularity, and physical appearance. I set my standards high and took action.

In my sophomore year I started exercising more. I spent extra time in the dance studio and rehearsal rooms. I did everything I could to keep up with the skinny, talented freshmen. I chased perfection for mile after mile on the treadmill, reading "expert" advice in magazines on how to "get slim by Sunday" and how to "be the life of every party." I looked to others to tell me whether I measured up. I hid my wild, curly hair and covered my freckles. I feared that if I let my true self show, I wouldn't be enough. I couldn't let my parents or high school friends think I was anything less than the star they expected me to be when I went away to college. I *had* to be the best at any cost.

My voice teacher pulled me into her office one afternoon, concerned about my sudden weight loss. "I'm fine," I assured her with a forced smile. "I'm just working out a lot for dance class right now. Trying to make it happen!" But I wasn't okay. I had an eating disorder. I couldn't get the image of the perfect girl I thought I was supposed to be to match who I actually was.

On the treadmill one day I suddenly felt my heart pounding erratically. The pit in my stomach from not eating and the stares from others in the gym came to a head in an anxiety attack. I sensed God saying to me, *Lara, you are going to die from this if you don't get off now.*

God wasn't telling me just to get off the treadmill; He was telling me to stop "chasing perfect"—or at least my idea of it—or die. I got off, went to the locker room, and stepped on the scale. At 5'9", I had shriveled to a mere 116 pounds.

I could barely get the words out when I called my mom. I was afraid to disappoint her, but I kept hearing the echo of God's gentle voice. I needed help.

The hardest part of breaking the chains of fear, control, and the chase for perfect is seeing that you need help. The second, equally hard, step is asking for it. Until that night I hadn't let anyone help me because *I was in control.* That day in the gym, my irregular heartbeat revealed the truth: I was chasing the uncatchable. My mom flew to Pittsburgh to get me, and college was put on hold. I was ashamed that I couldn't control my life and embarrassed to leave school, but the alternative was clear, and it was much worse than a bruised ego.

Do you feel like you are "chasing perfect" in some ways—attempting to measure up to an impossible standard?

Write down or say aloud how that is making you feel.

CRUSH THE "SHOULDS"

Perhaps you are thinking that what you are chasing isn't *that bad.* You don't have an eating disorder or any other major problem. And maybe you don't want to be perfect; you just want to live a good life and do your best. Still, you struggle at times, feeling like you are not enough. My chase for perfect may seem like the extreme, but the feeling of not measuring up is something shared by many of us—dare I say *all* of us?

I was doing what I thought I was supposed to do to be successful. In the race toward measuring up, we often don't realize we're being fueled by something harmful.

Give this question a chance, because it might ignite something you never expected: What are you really chasing?

Perhaps your struggle is not with chasing perfect. Maybe you're striving for success . . . for significance . . . for approval. What is the thing you are racing toward? Write it down or say it aloud.

Our chase for success so easily disguises itself as a "should"— because everyone around us is doing it. You *should* be working hard at the expense of time with your family if you want to be successful. You *should* be staying up late to get ahead if you want to make it. You *should* climb the success ladder now so you can live a joyful life when you retire.

You *should*, or you won't be enough.

Here's a wild question: What would happen if you threw out the "shoulds"? Who says you have to live by those rules? What if ending the chase and living on purpose means intentionally leaning in to what might feel imperfect? Maybe your laundry won't get done, or you will miss out on an opportunity for work. But your kids will be loved on, or you will have time for an undistracted dinner with your husband or a friend. Maybe you'll go to the park on your lunch break to get some fresh air instead of scarfing down a protein bar at your desk. Maybe you'll slow down enough to be able to listen to someone who really needs it.

Take a moment and imagine: What would happen if you threw out the *shoulds*? What would your life look like? Be specific.

Maybe a purposeful life means you'll have fewer followers on social media because you're not glued to your phone as much anymore. Maybe you'll get out in your garden, or paint, or have a long coffee date with someone and build a lasting connection. Maybe you'll call your grandma to tell her you love her and make her day. Maybe a purposeful life means you will make less money, but you'll find you have all you need.

But . . .

But there are bills to pay.

But I have responsibilities.

But it's complicated.

What *but* comes to your mind as soon as you think about surrendering control and taking a leap of faith? Fill in the blank below:

But _____.

Many of us fear that if we slow down even the tiniest bit, we will no longer be productive. We fear our lives will be meaningless if we aren't constantly striving for something bigger and better. Yet when we finally stop chasing those impossible standards and surrender our fears, we become truly productive in what matters. We experience genuine fulfillment: an imperfect yet intentional life, driven by a clear core purpose.

And you know what else? When we share our struggles on this journey to contentment, we ignite purposeful action in others as well. It creates a beautiful domino effect. People look at our lives and think, *She is imperfect and content, so maybe I could be too.*

So how do you get there?

Begin anywhere. Begin right where you are.

HOW ARE YOU?

You know that feeling you get when a good friend asks, "How are you?" You instantly tense up, not wanting to reveal the stuff that is weighing you down. You think, *I can't tell her. It's too much. I won't be able to stop if I start. I don't want to burden her. She'll think I'm crazy. I can't!*

"I'm fine," you quip.

Your friend asks again, "No, really . . . how *are* you?" The tone of her voice somehow makes you relax, and you just know: she wants the real answer, not the socially acceptable short version. Like honey to your soul, this genuine question makes you take in a deep, knowing breath. With your exhale, you pour out your heart. The emotion in your voice surprises you—you didn't realize you were carrying such a burden. Moments later, as if you've exhaled bricks, you feel a weight lifted off of your shoulders.

When people used to ask me how I was doing, I would slap

on a smile and give them a resounding, "Great!" But my closed body language and the tone in my voice told them otherwise.

What happens when you answer someone truthfully? You give the other person an unspoken invitation to do the same. Perfect says, "I'm fine," and the conversation dwindles. Perfect keeps it all bottled inside, snuffing out a possible life-changing connection between two souls. *Perfect is boring.* When a friend answers me honestly, I feel invited to let go and do the same, and life starts to happen. A connection is formed. Trust is built. Our lives are shared.

How about I go first?

I am feeling nervous right now. I am not a trained writer, nor do I work in professional ministry. But I want to help people know the truth because every day—in my work as a magazine publisher, during speaking engagements, at the grocery store and the airport—I meet countless women who feel held back from really *living.* Their fire has been put out, and we *need* their fire.

Most days I feel like I'm still twelve and wonder why God has me totally outside of my comfort zone: running a business, being a mom, writing these words to you, and doing many things I never thought I would do. I feel ordinary. I feel unprepared and in way over my head about a dozen times an hour. And that's the thing: I *am* unprepared and in over my head. But God does extraordinary things with our broken pieces when we give them to Him. He is real and good. And I know that God has given me a story to tell you. "You" meaning *you*. Not the collective "you" who may pick up this book, but *you*—the individual, courageous, beautiful person who is reading this right this second. The *you* who has a story and hidden passions and a deep desire for change . . . and there, I just took a big deep breath.

Now it's your turn. How are you? Why not stop for a minute and really think about it?

How are you?

Let that question settle for a moment longer than is comfortable for you. Now answer the question honestly, as you would to a close friend. Write it out or speak it.

THE CHASE

Life moves fast. So fast sometimes that we don't slow down enough to take stock of how we are doing. We think, *It doesn't matter how I feel right now. I must keep striving toward success! I'll feel things some other day.* Left with what seems like no choice but to press on, we do. Pushing our feelings aside, we grasp at the nearest sources of comfort or inspiration—magazines, TV, the Internet—filling our minds and hearts with the world's definition of what we should be, do, and think.

What sources of inspiration do you feed yourself? (Examples include social media, magazines, Scripture, books, blogs, friends, Pinterest, television, shopping, music.)

Which sources of inspiration are fueling you to live an intentional life?

Which sources of inspiration crush you at times, making you feel you must live up to impossible standards?

Over time the impossible standards we set for ourselves become the measuring stick for our worth. We start to believe that if we don't measure up, we aren't enough. We begin to feel worthless.

I did. Lost in the throes of busy, fueled by quick fixes that didn't fix anything at all, I believed the lies about who I was and wasn't supposed to be. I chased the standard of perfect.

Chasing perfect is comparing our worth with someone else's.

Chasing perfect makes us believe we are bad moms or bad wives or bad friends.

Chasing perfect makes us believe we are average and insignificant.

Chasing perfect makes us believe we will never be content.

Chasing perfect makes us believe we don't have enough friends, enough fun, or enough adventures.

Chasing perfect makes us believe we will never be successful.

Chasing perfect makes us do unreasonable things, like starve ourselves and buy things we can't afford, to measure up to our perceptions of others.

What has chasing perfect—striving for impossible standards—made *you* believe? Fill in the blank below:

Chasing perfect has made me believe _____ .

The next time we feel down, we race back to the very things that caused this emptiness in the first place. We buy, look, covet, and idolize again, and perhaps more than before. Our "inspiration" ends up intensifying the comparison and feelings of inadequacy that we were trying to escape. I'm speaking from my own heart, having fallen into these painful traps time and again.

The cycle continues until one day we find ourselves overwhelmed and overworked—or on a treadmill—thinking, *There must be a better way to live.*

There *is* a better way.

I thought my eating disorder would define me for the rest of my life. I feared my anxiety would hold me back from doing the things I was created to do. I feared I would *always* be stuck.

Are you there right now too? Do you fear that whatever it is holding you back—anxiety, fear, control, distrust, lack, or challenging circumstances—will always be there?

Be still, friend. Know that God's desire for you is a life of peace. He wants to free you from the chase. Wherever you are is exactly where you are supposed to be to ignite intentional change.

What would happen if you stopped chasing the uncatchable? What good could you do with your newfound time and energy?

The lies of perfection and shoulds tell us we aren't enough, but the truth paves a path for us to an abundant life of joy where we are more than enough. As my friend Emily Ley once told me, "I will hold myself to a standard of grace, not perfection."

Flaws, mistakes, and all—regardless of what you have done or where you have been—you matter. You were created for a purpose, and it's time to make it happen.

Making it happen means choosing
PURPOSE over PERFECT.

TAKE ACTION

▶ Write the following statement on a sticky note, and place it on your desk, refrigerator, or bathroom mirror:

I was created for a purpose, and it's time to make it happen!

▶ Go to www.LaraCasey.com/makeithappen and watch the video titled "Chasing Perfect."

2

MEET YOUR FEAR

Exchange your FEAR for faith.

I was driven by fear. I was afraid that I wouldn't be thin enough or talented enough and I would fail at college because I wasn't the best. And I would be unhappy for the rest of my life. And my parents would be disappointed, and I wouldn't have the glamorous life I wanted so badly, and no one would love me, and I would be *nothing*. I was also, ironically, afraid to succeed because I couldn't handle any more responsibilities or expectations.

I was afraid of surrendering control of my life because I thought everything would completely fall apart if I let go.

When I left college and came home to recover, I desperately wanted to find a way out of my fear and endless self-doubt. I gave myself permission to dream: *What if I wasn't driven by fear anymore? How would I feel? What would I do?*

If you are like me, you start to answer that question in your head, but something stops you. If fear didn't hold you back, the possibilities are so big they make you nervous. But we're just thinking here, not doing (yet), okay? What if fear didn't hold you back?

Imagine what life would be like if you exchanged your fear for faith. How would you feel? What would you be able to do? Write or speak aloud your ideas.

You can do this. Imagine the possibilities if you were to surrender your fear. Imagine how many people could be changed for the better. Imagine how your capacity to love others and use your gifts on purpose would multiply. Friend, what feels impossible is possible.

WHAT ARE YOU AFRAID OF?

Fear and I know each other well. We have spent holidays, summers, and long vacations together. We go way back. Fear is a strange thing, though, because it's not a *thing*. It's not something we can touch or pick up and remove from ourselves, though we would trade just about anything to do that, wouldn't we? I imagine a giant John Deere "Fear Extractor" rolling up into my driveway each day to take my heavy load away. Fear is not tangible, but it sure is real. It can feel like bricks on our hearts sometimes.

Do you feel that pressing weight right now? Let's start to define what your fear is and where it's coming from. This is going to be hard work, but we're clearing a path for purpose to take over every inch of you. This work will be worth it.

Fear can hold us back from making what matters happen. Fear can create a false reality where we feel threatened even if nothing has actually happened yet. What do you feel could be threatened in your life?

What are you scared of losing if your fears were to become reality or if you took the leap of faith that's on your heart?

Be specific and write it out. (Examples include self-worth, reputation, credibility, reliability, integrity, lifestyle, comfort, security.)

Many times, we deeply desire a change in our lives, but we fear that change might shake things up. We fear upsetting the status quo, causing trouble we are not prepared for. We fear that making a change will worsen our situations, so we find ourselves stuck. But there is a way out.

MEET YOUR FEAR

Fear isn't something to be crushed or ignored or buried. It will pop right back up if you try to stuff it away or pretend it's not there. Let's dig deeper and make a lasting change together. Meet your fear in order to know what to do with it.

When we take steps to meet our fears, it's much like meeting another person. To get to know someone, we give her our attention and engage her without distractions. We learn her subtleties—what makes her tick, where does she come from, what drives her? Getting to know our fears and what is causing them may involve asking others for advice, prayer, or wisdom. Understanding our fears may take help from a professional counselor, which is something I recommend.

As you meet your fears, listening to them in order to know where they are coming from, remember there is a difference between normal fear and abnormal fear. Normal fear is a very good thing. Normal fear keeps us from jumping off a cliff; abnormal fear keeps us from taking a leap of faith toward something that matters. Normal fear makes us question potentially damaging outcomes; abnormal fear makes us question our worth.

You may be thinking, *I don't want to meet my fear!* We hesitate (or run) because our fears feel *ugly.* We think, *I can't name that. That sounds crazy.* I hear you, friend. I've had all kinds of ugly hiding in the tender nooks of my heart. It's not easy to acknowledge, much less write or say. But it's time to do something about it. Remember the good that could happen if your fear didn't own you. You might finally do the things you were created to do. The things that could change the course of your life. The things that could inspire others and show them that they are deeply loved. The things that could change generations to come in your family. The things God purposed for you long ago. With those possibilities in mind, is it worth it to step into these hard places? I am here for you, and I will remind you as many times as you need to hear this: *living on purpose is worth stepping into all the hard stuff.*

When you get honest about what's holding you back, you open yourself to good change. Little by little, you exchange fear for a life of faith—a life where fear does not rule you but rather motivates you to dive deeper. A life that gets you and everyone around you fired up.

I have led a Making Things Happen workshop for the last seven years, helping people define what holds them back from taking action on what matters. Here are some of the real, honest fears expressed by the brave women I have spent time with:

- I am afraid if I pursue a job outside of my degree, my parents will be disappointed in me.
- I am afraid of losing my salary and security if I go full-time with my creative passion.
- I am afraid to start my business because I'm not an expert.
- I am afraid to be an at-home mom because I might lose my independence and passion for other things.
- I am afraid that my infertility makes me a disappointment and a failure as a woman.
- I am afraid to trust myself because of my past mistakes.
- I am afraid I will never have a career I love because I'm not as talented or smart as everyone else.
- I am afraid of surrendering my life to God because He might lead me where I don't want to go.
- I am afraid of putting myself out there because I will never measure up to the people I compare myself to.
- I am afraid of taking risks because people have told me I will fail. And if I fail, I will be nothing. I will be worthless.
- I am afraid of not being perfect in everything all the time because that's the expectation I've set for myself. Anything less than perfect feels like failure.

Do any of these hit home for you? If so, you are not alone. I've met thousands of women who echo these same feelings. I've felt many of these things too.

Are you ready to move toward a life of purpose? Then let's do this!

It's time to meet your fear.

Name your fears either on paper or out loud, describing what they are and why you feel that way. Personalize the sentence below with your own fear(s):

I am afraid of _____ *because* _____ .

Be specific. A general statement like "I am afraid of failure" doesn't clearly describe all that's pressing on your heart. Failing at what? Why do you feel that way?

As you continue to read and put words to what's holding you back, be equal parts kind to yourself *and* passionately clear, because you didn't buy this book to stay the same, *did you?* Be tender. Be bold. *The narrow path of purpose isn't always easy, but it is worth it.*

FEAR OF SUCCESS

When we look a level deeper, our greatest fear may actually be the very thing we are chasing: success. Why? If we finally realize our potential, we might be thrust into a life of responsibility that we can't handle. Hundreds of women have also shared these thoughts with me:

- I am afraid of trying because I might actually succeed.
- I am afraid of success because I might have to step out of my comfort zone.
- I am afraid of success because it might not be what I expect, and then I'll have to start over.
- I'm afraid of success because I believe I'll have to keep doing whatever I did to become successful nonstop *forever*, and I'll be trapped!
- I am afraid my success will be selfish.
- I am afraid of success because I know how addicted I can become to productivity and staying on top of things.

We fear success because it may invite a bigger opportunity for failure, it might take us away from our loved ones, or it might put us under the microscope of others. We fear success because we don't want to be sucked in to an even bigger chase for perfection.

So we decide that success is for everyone else, not us. We want to believe that only superheroes are able to accomplish extraordinary things. Because we see ourselves as ordinary, we shrink back and watch. We don't take risks because we think we are small. We don't do anything great because we think we weren't *made that way*.

———————————————————————————————

Take a closer look at the fear you have identified. Is it possible that you actually are afraid of success?

If so, use the prompt below to express your fear.

I am afraid to succeed because ————————————————.

Now allow yourself to take a moment to imagine what would happen if you let go of that fear—and experienced the success you're longing for. What would your life look like? What potential positive effect could your success have on others as well?

Throughout the Bible, God chose ordinary and imperfect people—fishermen, shepherds, and farmers—to do astounding things. Even though we are ordinary, God can make the impossible possible when we humble ourselves and surrender our fears to Him. God does not need you to be a superhero in order to use you for His great purposes. He just needs your humble, willing heart.

THE GOOD FEAR

There *is* something different about people who live on purpose, though. It's the same thing I see in my friend Kristin, who recently lost her baby girl, Sophia, but is teaching others how to find joy amid great loss. It's the same thing I see in my editor friend who fights for great stories to be told that transform people's lives. It's the same thing I see in my friend Hannah, who left love letters all over New York City, sparking the international movement MoreLoveLetters.com, which encourages millions through the personal and poignant gift of a handwritten letter. It's the same thing I see in my friend Jimmy Wayne, who walked halfway across the United States to raise awareness for homeless teens who age out of foster care. These friends walk the walk—against great odds—because their hearts belong to something bigger than them.

To fear something means you respect it. It has power. It has influence on your life. I know that sounds backward—how can we respect something we fear? But think about it this way: if you fear what other people think, that means you respect them so much that their opinions matter. You fear disappointing them. If you fear failing as a mom, then you respect the role of motherhood so much that you want to be your best. If you fear not succeeding in your career, then the desire to succeed has influence on you.

The thing we fear is what we are giving power to in our lives. It's what we are allowing to influence us.

Proverbs 31 describes a woman who "can laugh at the days to come" (v. 25). She has no fear about the future, not because her life is guaranteed to be perfect or because she was born a superhuman but because she knows and trusts in something bigger than her. When we believe in something more powerful than elusive perfection, we develop the courage to bid our fears farewell. The chase ends, and real life begins.

The Proverbs 31 woman is hardworking, a savvy businesswoman, a loving homemaker, a wise mother, and praised by her husband and children. It's easy to read the first twenty-nine verses and think, *I will never measure up to that!* Read verse 30, though, and you see the truth: "Charm is deceptive, and beauty is fleeting; but a woman who fears the LORD is to be praised." The reason the Proverbs 31 woman was able to develop these characteristics over the course of her lifetime was because her strength was not her own. The only thing that was perfect about her was God's transformative power.

We are going to have fear in our lives, but the fear of the Lord releases the hold that all other fears have on us. Fear motivates us to make decisions in order to get something we want.

of the Lord changes what we want. The fear of the Lord—giving Him respect and influence over our lives above all else—is a positive fear that refines our hearts, pushing us to make what really matters happen. It's a fear that inspires good choices and bold leaps of faith. The fear of God enables us to live a life of purpose in which our paralyzing fears are replaced with trust in His wisdom.

I need daily reminders that God is God. He is in control so I don't have to be. He has a plan that is far better than mine. My role is to follow Him, saying, *I trust You. I surrender my fear and my ways. I take You at Your Word.* His ways free me from fear and the chase for perfection.

Is fear holding you back from living on purpose? Let your faith speak louder than your crushing fears. Find freedom by loving God and surrendering all your fears to Him. Then what previously was scary will no longer be scary—because you will have met your fears and given them over to God, trusting in the fact that God is *God* and He is leading you to where you need to go.

Making it happen means meeting your FEAR.

TAKE ACTION

▶ Like the Proverbs 31 woman, *you* can laugh without fear of the future. Revisit the fears you met earlier in the chapter.

Surrender them to God, and then trust God to lead you where you need to go.

▶ Do something small that you have been afraid of doing—something you can do in the next five minutes. Some ideas: send that e-mail you've been putting off, ask that question you've been wanting to ask, start that project, say you're sorry, let something go. Take the first tiny step! Say it, send it, start it, write it, make the call, dive in. Life is too short to let fear hold you back.

3

END THE EXTREMES

Success and BALANCE aren't opposites.

The therapist held his Snickers bar four inches from my face and asked how it made me feel. He said, "If you can learn to be comfortable eating a Snickers bar, you will be cured." Even I knew that my battle in college wasn't with food itself—that's just what I chose to control in my life.

That was the first and last session I went to with that particular therapist, but it taught me something: *the battle is always bigger than what it looks like on the surface.* You can clean your house from top to bottom, get new plants, buy new furniture, or cover your walls with a fresh coat of paint, but that won't transform the heart living inside those walls. Surface changes may make you feel new and refreshed but only for a short while. I didn't need to get comfortable eating a Snickers bar; I needed to get comfortable in my own skin. I needed a heart change.

But how was I supposed to be happy in my body when I was crushed by the shame of not feeling good enough? I believed my body was imperfect and hindering me from success. The idea of accepting myself seemed like accepting defeat and a life of mediocrity. I didn't want to accept where I was. I wanted out!

Just fix yourself. Just be happy. Just accept where you are. Easier said than done, right?

What about you? How do these statements make you feel?

- Just be happy where you are.
- Just be okay with yourself.
- Accept what you cannot change.

Do those statements help you—or make you feel frustrated and hopeless?

You want to know a freeing truth? It's okay *not* to be happy where you are sometimes. But don't let your unhappiness make you ungrateful or resentful. Let it empower you toward positive change. Let it help you dig deeper and find lasting contentment.

It's okay to be restless, knowing there is more you are meant to do, but don't allow it to stop you from living right *now*. Let that feeling spur you to action and curious exploration.

And it's okay to want to change the things that feel impossible. Maybe you *can* change, but you are unsure of what to do. Let that doubt lead you forward. Let the unrest reveal your next move.

When I left college to get help, I didn't think it was okay to feel unrest. People kept saying, "Just be happy where you are." But I wanted to be happy in my own skin and still realize my potential in life. I wanted to find balance *and* still be successful. *How come no one can tell me how to do that?* I was angry at everyone around me for not having a solution that seemed reasonable.

Have you been asking that same question?

How can we live healthy, intentional hours *and* reach our fullest potential?

We ask the question as if balance and success are opposites, warring against each other. As if there are only two options: find balance and be mediocre, or be successful and lose your time and relationships. But true success and balance are not opposites; they are the same.

I can see the giant question mark flashing over your head right now. I know it may be hard to imagine. It was for me. The idea frustrated me because it didn't make sense at first. I thought balance meant living a slower life and success meant living a faster life. How could these two extremes exist together? The answer lies in coming to know what true success and balance are.

Take a few minutes to answer these questions:

- What is your definition of balance?
- What would your life look and feel like if you had balance?
- What is your definition of success?
- What would your life look and feel like if you had success?

Now here's the crazy question: What would your life look like if you had *both*?

Maybe you do have both in some ways. Or maybe you are like me back then, believing that success had to be all or nothing. Balance got edged out, because how could they coexist?

GO BIG OR GO HOME

In striving for success—however we define *success*—many of us go to extremes. We push ourselves by working 24-7, unhealthy dieting, compulsive cleaning, constant connectivity, or extreme spending. We cheer, "Go big or go home!" When everyone around us is racing to the top, the idea of being in the middle makes us worry about being left behind or forgotten, doesn't it?

The go-big-or-go-home mind-set gives you only two options: give 110 percent and be perfect, or make one mistake and be a failure. Just as black and white is often easier to understand than gray, an extreme position can seem easier than balance. We find a sense of security in always knowing the answer when faced with a decision: I *never* eat chocolate; I can *never* go home from the office early; I *always* have to be glued to my phone, or I might miss something.

Moderation isn't an option because we fear losing control.

Are you there right now? Do you feel like you will be left behind in the dust if you don't press forward? Are your pushing yourself to unhealthy extremes in your quest for success?

It's okay to admit it. Owning where we are allows us to step into life-altering change. If the burden of striving feels heavy, let it go, friend. Let it all go. Fight the urge to decide that what you are feeling right now is *wrong*. The goal is not to condemn yourself but to get clarity that will spur you on to positive action. Compassionately write what you are feeling.

Here's what I felt: I was driven and impulsive. If I was going to get healthy, I was going to be the healthiest. If I found a shampoo I liked, I'd buy five bottles. If I was given a role I loved, I threw my whole self into becoming the character. If I read one line of a book and liked it, I'd buy every book from that author. I couldn't just buy one of something, put one foot in, or go halfway. I went all in, all the time. Because that's what successful people do, right?

A BUMPY-SCARY-EXTREME CARRIAGE RIDE

It's ironic that roller coasters have the word *coast* in them, as if to imply they take us on a smooth, gliding ride. I hereby give the roller coasters in our lives a more appropriate title: *bumpy-scary-extreme carriages*. Extremes can only be sustained for a short time before they display the laws of physics: what goes up must come down.

I wanted to *fix* myself so I could get back on track with pursuing my dreams. Books and my parents and my new therapist kept telling me, "Just let go and eat!" Exhausted and angry, I felt like I had hit a dead end. *Okay, fine! If this doesn't work, I will blame all of you.* I resentfully let go of control and, like a bumpy-scary-extreme carriage roaring down a steep incline without any brakes, things quickly got out of hand. I went through the McDonald's drive-through to get an ice cream cone. I was at Burger King ten minutes later. And at a restaurant ten minutes after that. At the grocery store. At the mini-mart. It was as if someone had flipped a switch, and suddenly I was going in the opposite direction. All the things I had deprived myself of were my new obsessions. I didn't know how to do moderation.

It was as messy as it sounds. Under all the mess, though, was a nineteen-year-old heart that just wanted to be whole.

My emotional chaos was growing. I went back to school, but I didn't talk to anyone about how I felt or about my anorexia. I didn't want people watching me or questioning my eating; I just wanted to be normal. And I tried, *hard*. I went to therapy appointments twice a week at an outpatient eating disorders clinic. Much to the relief of my parents and therapist, I started gaining weight. It seemed I was recovering well.

Soon, though, the weight gain made me feel out of control. In my mind, the numbers were alarming. I was recovering the weight far too quickly for my emotions to catch up. Shame screamed at me day and night, *You will never be enough.* I spiraled downward. I skipped therapy sessions. I didn't want to feel; I wanted to be numb. I started partying, trying to find momentary happiness. I defiantly bought clothes I didn't need and piles of self-help books I never read with money my parents had generously given me for basic needs. I tried to fill the holes in my soul with whatever promised a quick patch: compliments, possessions, and food. In five months, I gained more than fifty pounds.

It all happened so fast. I had swung from one extreme to the other, but the same thing was driving those ups and downs: mounting shame. Not feeling like I'd ever be enough.

What about you? When will you finally feel like you are enough? Fill in the blanks below:

*I don't feel*_____*enough.*

I will be enough when _____.

Can we pause here for a moment?

My daughter, Grace, is two and a half. No matter what she's doing—working a puzzle, eating a snack, or figuring out how to stuff all her toys in her Sunday school backpack—the moment she sees me come down from my office to the kitchen, she drops everything and runs to me with open arms. "Mommeeeee!" It doesn't matter what she was doing. She's not worried about the past or the future. She's just happy *being*.

She has been asking me some pretty poignant questions lately. For example:

- "Mommy, are we all babies?"
- "Mommy, did you know that honeys like bees?"
- "Mommy, can I make poop and pee at the same time?"

Her questions make me laugh inside, but I try to keep a straight face because she really wants to know.

Now imagine her asking me this question: "Mommy, am I enough?"

What would you say?

- "No, not until you get into an Ivy League school."
- "No, not until you are perfectly thin and beautiful."
- "No, not until you have enough money in your bank account."

You may be cringing reading this. The very thought of telling a wide-eyed toddler she is not enough is outrageous and cruel.

Why should we feel differently about how we treat ourselves?

Somewhere between the hangovers and distracted performances at school and shopping bags full of things I couldn't afford, I hit rock bottom. In a mess of tears in my room, I cracked open a Bible that my grandpa had given me. I flipped to a random page, not having any idea where to start. As I read a verse or two, my mind started spinning with questions and negative thoughts:

- *Who am I? Nothing.*
- *What is my purpose? I don't have one and I will never find it.*
- *Why do I feel so empty? I don't know. I will never be fulfilled.*

I wanted to feel alive. I wanted to be on the right path, but I couldn't get the self-defeating thoughts to stop. Then I read these words: "Therefore, if anyone is in Christ, the new creation has come: The old has gone, the new is here!" (2 Cor. 5:17). I so badly wanted to be made completely new. Little by little over the next decade, God helped me replace the lies I had believed with truths.

REPLACING LIES

Here are some common lies we feed ourselves:

- I am not good enough.
- I will never be successful.
- I am destined to fail.
- There is no reason why anyone should like me.
- I am too bad of a person to have a relationship with God.
- I am not smart enough, talented enough, pretty enough.
- I am no one.

What negative chatter swims in your head day after day? Which lie(s) have you been telling yourself lately? Write down these thoughts.

My lies at the time threatened to crush me, but God's truth was aimed at exposing them:

- *The lie:* Your life is out of control. Everyone thinks you are a failure. Nobody likes you.
- *The truth:* God is for you. "If God is for us, who can be against us?" (Rom. 8:31).

- *The lie:* You will never be successful. You will never be beautiful. You will never do anything great.
- *The truth:* God made you for good reasons. "For we are God's handiwork, created in Christ Jesus to do good works, which God prepared in advance for us to do" (Eph. 2:10).

- *The lie:* You are alone. No one understands what you are going through.
- *The truth:* You are not alone. God understands completely. "For we do not have a high priest who is unable to empathize with our weaknesses, but we have one who has been tempted in every way, just as we are— yet he did not sin" (Heb. 4:15).

- *The lie:* You will never be free of this. It will haunt you for the rest of your life.
- *The truth:* The best is yet to come. "I remain confident of this: I will see the goodness of the Lord in the land of the living. Wait for the Lord; be strong and take heart and wait for the Lord" (Ps. 27:13–14).

Despite the verses I read, I was still hesitant. Part of me wanted to continue believing the lies because they meant I didn't have to try to be anything. I could hide. But God wired us to be *something* for Him. Not for our own gain or praise, but all for Him. The restlessness you may feel is there for a reason, calling you to step into the truth. For me, it was time to break free. But how?

I thought it was impossible for my life to change, and then I read this: "With man this is impossible, but with God all things are possible" (Matt. 19:26).

All things? Really? *How?* I wanted the impossible to happen in my life. I kept asking questions and looking for the answers.

Revisit your answer to the last question—the lie(s) you have been telling yourself lately. Now go to www.openbible.info/topics, type in the issue you're struggling with (for example, *value, loneliness,* or *failure*), and see what God's Word has to say about it. Read each verse in context.

In the space below, write out the lie you've believed—and then replace that lie with the reality of God's truth. This rewiring of our hearts is hard work, and I hope it brings you a jolt of clarity as it did—and continues to do—for me.

The lie:

The truth:

GET OFF THE ROLLER COASTER

We can slow down or stop the roller coaster, but if we don't get out of that metal bullet to start pursuing a life of purpose, we may be tempted by the thrill once again. Up and down I had gone. It was time to *get off.*

If you want change, choose it. Step into the hard stuff in order to get to the good stuff. I recommitted to my therapy sessions to sort through the mess in my heart. My therapist encouraged me to envision a life without extremes, where the chains of striving for perfection and the crushing shame of not being enough were broken. A place of freedom. A place of purpose. A place where I belonged. A place where I was fully enough.

I closed my eyes and was surprised by what I immediately pictured: Grandpa. But he had such an ordinary life. He worked at JCPenney, tended his garden, and sold flour door-to-door. He preached and led music in church. I wanted so much more

36

than that. I wanted a glamorous life with luxuries and travel and comfort.

But what if I lived like Grandpa—what would that look like? What if I started to believe all the verses I was reading in the Bible? Would I have to live a radically different life? What if I went to church? Would people judge me? How would I even find a church, or have time for it?

Grandpa's life didn't seem like much on the outside, but he had something I wanted, something I craved. Grandpa wasn't chasing perfect or controlled by fear—he was compelled by something else. Something that made him know, without doubt, that he was enough. Grandpa knew that the path to true success ended extremes and brought contentment. He knew the secret to living in plenty or little that Paul describes in Philippians 4:13, the same verse that is now etched in the tiniest letters inside my wedding band: "For I can do everything through Christ, who gives me strength" (NLT).

Making it happen means ending the EXTREMES.

TAKE ACTION

▶ What extremes have you experienced in the past? What extremes do you feel pressured to strive for now? Define your extremes in order to step off the bumpy-scary-extreme carriage and move toward a life of contentment. Write them out so you can see them.

▶ Now write out why you think you feel pressured to go to these extremes. Many times, the thing we go to extremes for is not the thing we most need. For example, when we strive for popularity, we don't want simply to increase the number of people we know; we may want to feel loved. When we follow unhealthy diets, we may really be trying to gain control in our lives over something deeper than a number on a scale. When we shop compulsively, we often don't need more clothes or office supplies; we may be needing to feel accepted or _____ (fill in whatever it might be for you). What are you really craving? Write it out in detail.

▶ Go to www.LaraCasey.com/makeithappen and print a free Psalm 23 art print for your home or office (feel free to print one to encourage a friend too) to remind you where to find peace when you feel pulled to extremes or find yourself striving.

4

FIND AN ANCHOR

Choose what MATTERS.

My prayers were totally one-sided at first. They weren't conversations at all. I would pray things like, "God, make me perfect. Make me the best. Help me control my eating. Make that guy like me. Change me so people will like me more." Then I would get frustrated waiting for Him to answer. I started thinking, *God, I'm talking to You—why aren't You answering me?*

I wanted to have faith, but . . .

My list of buts was *long.*

- But I had no idea where to start.
- But the Bible was confusing.
- But finding a church seemed overwhelming.
- But my friends didn't believe.
- But my past was too tainted. I'd been too bad.
- But I thought faith would just make my life harder.

Crazy question time: *What if our hesitations aren't roadblocks but starting points?* What if leaning in to these sticky feelings will help us find out the real truth—the real path to contentment, purpose, and being enough? And what if finding that path is really simple?

In my college room that day, I read these words: "I am the way and the truth and the life" (John 14:6). I wanted someone to show me the way, and I wanted a new life, a fresh start. I decided to pray something that felt a little scary because I didn't totally know what it meant: "Please, God, show me the way."

My simple prayer was an act of surrender. I chose to let go of my ways in exchange for an unknown path I hoped would be better.

If you've never done it before, talking to God can feel weird. At first you may feel like you are having a conversation with the air or talking to yourself. It can even feel like an awkward first date. *Am I saying the right things? Does He like me? What is He thinking right now?* The more time you and God spend together, though, whether you share many words or just a few, the closer you grow. Whatever prayer is on your heart, give it breath.

Stop a moment and give breath to the prayer that's on your heart right now. You can even jot it in the margin of this book. It doesn't have to be long or fancy—just from your heart.

If you're new to prayer and don't know where to start, feel free to say the same simple prayer I did: "Please, God, show me the way."

I wrote Bible verses on brightly colored index cards and started putting them all over my room. Still looking for a quick fix, though, I would bounce from chapter to chapter and read whatever verse popped out—whatever made me feel good at the time—instead of full chapters that explained the context of those words. I didn't know any better. I didn't have Christian friends or a church; it was just me alone in my room, searching for answers. I wanted someone to hand me the "How to Be a Christian" cheat sheet so I could learn the rules.

But faith is not about following rules. It's about letting God change your heart and then living in response to that heart change.

LIVING IN TWO WORLDS

The next semester I took a religion class and made some friends who invited me to church. These new friends showed me what faith was really about. They were joyful and authentic. They studied the Bible and prayed with me through my endless doubts and questions. And they didn't judge me; they loved me as I was. This was what I was looking for. They had what Grandpa had. They had God—the real God who loves us in all our mess.

When you see faith in action—real, raw, active faith—it's powerful. I wanted to live like my new friends. I wanted to live on purpose. I wanted an anchor. So I surrendered and said, *God, I choose to follow You. I want to start fresh and be on a path to something that matters.* I said yes to a new life with God and was baptized on a cool night in March, just as the last frost of the winter was lifting.

"New life" is a funny thing, though. You expect it to be all rainbows and halos after you say yes to God, but spiritual birth is much like our physical births. Immediately after we are born, we are fully reliant on our parents to care for us and nurture us. If we were to put toddlers into college, what would happen? They wouldn't know how to use the potty, much less handle the rigors of academia. I was in the infant stages of my faith, still easily influenced by the world.

I wanted my life to be truly new, but my circumstances outside of church remained the same. I had to work hard not to fall back into the trap of negative self-talk during school performances and critiques. I fought to remember the truths God was rewriting in my heart. There were days I felt like throwing in the towel and quitting theater altogether. Those days I held fast to God as my anchor, no matter how much the waves battered me, because the alternative was to go back to the way my life was.

Walking out of class one September morning, I glanced at my cell phone to see five missed calls from my mom. I called her back and heard, "Lara, a plane has hit the World Trade Center—and another—and there is one headed to Pittsburgh!" I walked into the student center to see CNN broadcasting live on a giant screen, horrifying scenes flashing before my eyes. My cell phone signal died as the networks were overloaded.

A few days later our department assembled to talk about the tragedy. I stood up and said, without hesitation, that we needed to "pray and turn to God. He has all the answers." I sat down, feeling a mix of relief and embarrassment. *Where did those words come from?* Well, they kept coming.

I started a prayer group that met in a tiny rehearsal room in the drama department. Two friends would meet with me at lunch to pray. I started studying the Bible with a few classmates, trying to help them find comfort in God too. I was grateful to be alive and learning how to live like a believer.

FACING OPPOSITION

Later that semester our final senior show was announced. There were parts of the script that made me feel uncomfortable. It reminded me of the life I had left behind. I didn't want my mind and heart involved in anything that would pull me away from my new faith, so I told my adviser I couldn't do the show. Even if it was just a play, I didn't want to glorify something that God wouldn't love. I didn't want to take a step back into the life where I had almost killed myself chasing unattainable perfection. I wouldn't go back to feeling alone and scared while partying and eating to stuff my feelings away. I was on a new path.

The next thing I knew, the faculty told me I had to do the play to graduate. I cried and told them I couldn't. People started wondering why I was "so religious" all of a sudden. The waves crashed harder. I felt confused as to why God would lead me to such opposition. I felt like I couldn't win, no matter what I did. Getting healthy didn't work, quick recovery didn't work, partying didn't work, and now faith was starting to make me feel alone and depressed.

Thanks to a few teachers petitioning on my behalf, I was given an alternate assignment. I was cast in a tiny play with some younger students. It was a blessing in disguise, and I made some great new friends, but it still felt like a punishment.

Second semester of senior year, the big questions loomed: *What am I going to do with my life after school? How will I support myself? Is this the path You want me to take, God?* Immediately after graduation, we would perform for agents in Los Angeles and New York, and they would decide, based on our two-minute performances, if they would sign us.

It seemed I had no other career options. Theater was what

...d done with my entire life. How could I start over? But my restlessness grew as graduation neared. Was I supposed to take this path that seemed expected? Perhaps God had another plan. Perhaps He has an unexpected plan for you too.

Making it happen means holding fast to the ANCHOR.

TAKE ACTION

▶ Have you ever felt tossed back and forth, trying to please people in different worlds, searching for an anchor to hold you steady? Write out your experience.

▶ Surround yourself with reminders of what matters for the times when the waves come crashing. Some ideas: post bright cards with favorite Bible verses on your bathroom mirror or office bulletin board, keep a Bible open on your kitchen counter, or go to www.LaraCasey.com /makeithappen and print out a "What Matters Most" list to fill out and post on your fridge or in a place you will see often.

5

DECIDE YOU CAN

*Believe in the Possibilities
You can't yet see.*

Everything I owned was packed in my car as I searched for parking in midtown Manhattan. My agent sent me on an audition the same day I moved to New York. Something didn't feel right as I, a 5'9" redhead, stepped into a room with a dozen 5' brunettes. My agent had told me this was a first-round audition for the young female lead in *Mamma Mia!* on Broadway. However, I soon realized this was the callback, and I was as odd in that bunch as a turkey in a hen house. I don't even remember what I sang or what happened in that room. I just remember feeling, from the moment I set foot on that island, that I was not where I was supposed to be.

My faith had dwindled as I spent every waking moment trying to "make it" in the New York acting world. But I was growing tired of auditioning, hoping to make the cut. I was in a city of millions of people, yet I felt alone. I ignored calls from my agent and my parents. I gained weight and started to feel depressed. *What's wrong with me? Why can't I just control my life?*

I felt like I had nowhere to turn: my agent didn't get me; my parents didn't understand; my friends from college were all hustling to get jobs. I felt distant from God, and I didn't have Christian friends there to support me and reel me back in.

One cold November morning, with the light barely coming up over the East River in my tiny apartment on Roosevelt Island, the phone rang. "Lara . . ." My mom's voice shook on the other line. "Grandpa Cecil passed away." My breath left me for a moment. There were no tears, though. Warm peace washed over me as I pictured Grandpa finally meeting the God he dearly loved. No pain, no struggle—just he and his Maker. That morning, he had eaten a big piece of chocolate cake for breakfast and then quietly passed from this life to life eternal.

At his funeral we all felt compelled to share from our hearts about Grandpa. My mom shared how he had taught her to pray. My dad told of his simple life, making much of God and very little of himself. Grandpa's friend Louis spoke of his devotion to serving the church. And I shared about my last conversation with Grandpa on a visit home.

My parents had gone out to dinner, and I stayed home to be with Grandpa. I brought him his favorite treat: vanilla ice cream. He listened patiently as I told him about the things that were on my mind. I asked him questions like, "What is the most important thing to know about life?" and "What is heaven going to be like?" The answers were there in his kind eyes long before I asked the questions: *Lara, read the Bible. God has all the answers.*

He didn't have a flashy title or lots of money, and he didn't leave much behind in the world except chicken-scratched notes in the margins of his Bible. He wasn't perfect or the best at anything, but he changed people with his humble heart. We felt Jesus through his love and his smile.

Grandpa's legacy, alive in the hearts of all who knew and loved him, changed me too.

CLOSING ONE DOOR, OPENING ANOTHER

I knew what I had to do. I had to surrender my fear and open myself to the unknown—to new possibilities. I had to close one door in order for another one to open.

Not knowing how I would pay off my college debt or my bills, I went back to New York and left theater for good. I walked into my agent's office, told him I was done, and walked out to a new life. I didn't have any idea what lay ahead or what to do next, but I knew what I *wasn't* going to do. I couldn't sit and let the days of my life tick away anymore, waiting for the perfect role. I was tired of waiting for life to start once I "made it." I wanted to help other people and do something with my life that left a legacy like Grandpa's, pointing people to what matters. I didn't know how that was going to happen, but I knew why.

What do you sense God is saying to you about your next step in creating a life of purpose? Do you stay, or do you go?

Take a moment to ask God for wisdom. The Bible says, "If you don't know what you're doing, pray to the Father. He loves to help" (James 1:5 MSG). If you're not sure whether to stay or go in your specific situation, pray and ask God to help you know what to do. Prayer is an action step, friend. Perhaps the very best one.

THE WAITING PLACE

Sometimes it is good to stay and press into our challenging circumstances. Sometimes the hard stuff we're in is exactly where God wants us to be in order to strengthen us. Waiting on God can refine us and build our faith. Some of the best things in life come with patient waiting and a period of growth. Friend, *this season of waiting might be your time of ripening.*

But there is a difference between patiently waiting on God—being open to and changed by the nutrients He gives you in challenges—and waiting because of fear.

We might fear rejection, failure, or hard work. We want to be sure that our actions will be successful, and without such certainty, we cannot make decisions. We are paralyzed by worry. We get stuck, waiting for a good feeling in order to make a decision. If it *feels* right, we take action. But many times the right decision doesn't feel good. Most of the wisest decisions I've made in my life have felt downright scary. They did not feel logical or intuitive, but when I did things God's way, He led me in the right direction. His plans are bigger than mine, so they tend to pull me out of my feel-good zone. Sometimes He purposefully brings us to the edge of the cliff so we will choose Him over our fears.

Maybe this challenging time or place is meant for your good. Maybe this season of waiting is really a season of preparation, getting you ready for something better. Something you never expected.

Are you in a season of waiting right now? If so, *why* are you waiting? To dig deeper and find out the real reason you've been waiting to take the leap to make it happen, ask yourself the following questions:

- Am I waiting on God—trusting in His timing and being open to His work in my life? Am I at peace in my current situation and challenges, actively expecting God to work through them to work out His purposes in my life?
- Am I waiting because of fear—paralyzed by worry or anxiety about the future? Am I waiting to make decisions that could move me forward into a life of purpose because I fear rejection, failure, or hard work?

It's okay to admit that you're waiting because of fear or having a hard time trusting God's timing and plans. I've been there a trillion times. Put words to how you are feeling and tell God, instead of letting fear or hesitations put out your fire any longer. If you feel restless or fearful, remember: lean in, be honest, and know God is God. He will guide you through this. Always.

Sometimes we must submit to the waiting and keep our hearts open to what it will teach us. And sometimes we must act on the clarity God gives us, even when it doesn't make sense. We must get on with our lives! My decision to leave theater didn't feel good—in fact, it felt reckless. But the alternative for me was to stay stuck. There was nothing wrong with acting itself, but I felt pulled to something different. Just one problem: I had no idea what that thing was.

HUMILITY IS WHERE CHANGE STARTS

After giving up my acting aspirations, my life was now open, which was partly terrifying and partly freeing. I didn't know where to start, so I just started somewhere. I waited tables to pay the bills and joined a gym. I wanted to feel healthy and ready for whatever was ahead in my blank-slate life. I knew I had to do *something* positive.

I'd go to the gym late at night, trying to avoid people. During those nights at the gym in the city that never sleeps, I would see a thick, muscle-clad trainer with tight braids and piercing eyes working with clients. I'd watch the clients walk in for their sessions with him looking deflated and tired, much like me. But when they left, there were springs in their steps and smiles on their faces. One lady would even sing on the way out. Whatever magic potion he was feeding people, I wanted it super-sized. So one night I walked up to him and asked him to train me.

In our first session he put a forty-five-pound bar in my hands. He walked me through how to do a slow, controlled squat and then said, "Okay, go." It looked easy, and the bar didn't seem heavy. *How hard can this be?* Ray had this evil laugh that I eventually grew to love. He cackled as he guided me through each squat, seeing my growing discomfort with every rep. My knees nearly gave out, and my muscles started to burn after just three squats.

The first thing Ray taught me was that *being humbled is where change starts.*

There is a moment when we are given a choice: let our egos run the show, or surrender our fears and be humbled. The latter is how we make it happen. The times I have been knocked off my feet, realizing I am weak or have no idea what I'm doing, have been catalysts for powerful growth.

Have you learned more from the times you've been humbled than the times you succeeded? I sure have. The times I have felt I had no idea what I was doing—the times that knocked me off my feet—have been the times I grew the most.

Think back on a time you failed or felt humbled. How did you grow from the experience?

Write this somewhere where you will see it often:

Failure is fertilizer.

The morning after my first workout with Ray, I groaned as I bent forward to spit my toothpaste in the sink. *Why did I subject myself to this?* Ray, however, had a plan. A few days later I hesitantly walked into the gym for my second session. I had given myself an audible pep talk on the subway ride over—totally normal in NYC—expecting more torture and humiliation. He put the same bar in my hands, had me perfectly position every muscle . . . and then added ten-pound weights to each side.

"Yeah, right!" I protested. "There's no way I can do *more!*"

Silence. And then this: "You are far more capable than you think, Lara. You *can* do this," he said in a powerful whisper that could have cut right through the solid iron in my hands.

Then he repeated these words loudly and with fiery conviction, as if in that moment he saw through my layers of hurt and heartache to a strong, confident me: "Decide that you can."

Decide that you can.

Ray's gift wasn't training people's muscles; it was helping them surrender their fears. He would listen to self-doubt without judgment and then guide them through the process of replacing it with confidence. Ray knew I had the strength to do it, but my fear was telling me otherwise. My self-imposed limitations had me stuck in disbelief.

How many times have you accepted defeat before even *trying*? We are so quick to limit ourselves, deciding who we are and who we aren't and that's it. We define our identities—our strengths, weaknesses, likes, dislikes, and beliefs—but this rigid defining can hinder us from seeing the potential that God sees. We stay in our little identity boxes, not allowing ourselves to be stretched or challenged. We accept the world's made-up rules for who we are supposed to be, and we believe we cannot break those rules.

What about you? How many times have you accepted defeat before even *trying*? What have you unknowingly decided that you cannot do? Write down your thoughts or speak them aloud.

I had decided I wasn't strong enough. I was told in college that I was "sensitive," so I believed that meant I was weak. I had decided that lifting weights was manly and not something girls did. And I had never lifted that much weight before, so I had decided I wasn't capable.

Ray's belief in what I couldn't see made me brave.

I exchanged my fear for belief, kicking the negativity out of my head as I pushed and pushed and . . . there I was, standing straight up with the iron barbell securely in my hands. I felt like

I had sprouted wings. In that moment, and countless like it to follow, I realized I was capable of more than I thought.

Humility creates an opportunity for strength when we choose to step outside our identity boxes and believe in possibilities not yet seen. Possibilities that open us to give more, create more, and see more good.

Allow yourself to imagine the possibilities if you were to crush your own little identity box. What would happen if you broke all the rules? If you were capable of doing the very thing you think you cannot do, how would you be able to thrive—and to help others? List the possibilities on paper. Be specific.

Decide today to believe in possibilities not yet seen.

LEADING WHILE LEARNING

Over the next weeks of training, I felt a new confidence. I learned that opening myself to twitching muscles and sore limbs gave way to change. Soreness gave way to strength. Ray also taught me how to use food as fuel, seeing it as a positive energy source instead of something that needed restrictive control. I felt hope.

As my own transformation started to unfold, I discovered a deep desire to help people transform themselves too. I wanted people to know they were enough. I wanted to help other women not fall into the traps I had fallen into during college, constantly striving for outer perfection instead of inner strength.

Seeing my progress and my passion, Ray encouraged me to become a personal trainer. The doubt poured in: *I am not* prepared, good enough, or smart enough. *I don't have a degree in exercise science. I am still the trainee. How can I lead while I am still learning?* His reply: "Because helping people is worth far more than your doubts. Decide that you can."

Six months after walking up to Ray in the gym, I took my first National Academy of Sports Medicine exam. It was far outside my identity box. It felt a little crazy. But I wanted to make this happen—not just for me but for the potential I saw to ignite change in others. My life could *mean something.*

I trudged through the New York snow early one morning and walked up to Ray in the middle of one of his sessions. I smiled. He beamed back as I said the two words that changed the course of my life: "I passed."

Making it happen means
deciding that YOU CAN!

TAKE ACTION

▶ What things are on your heart to do that feel outside of your "identity box?" Write them out. Then go to openbible .info/topics/identity and read about what God desires our identities to be. Read these verses in context and examine whether the things on your list align with God's heart.

► What decisions in your life are you afraid to make right now? What doors do you want to close? Write out the fears or circumstances that are holding you back from making a decision to take a step forward into making it happen.

► Decide that you can. Go to www.LaraCasey.com /makeithappen and print out the "I CAN" declaration or fill it in below:

Today is the day that everything changes.
Today I break the rules about who I am supposed to be and take action on who God made me to be.
Today I choose to take action on _____.
God is my strength. He never fails.
Taking action on this is worth it because

_____.

Let's do this!

6

LET IT GO

Endings can be new beginnings.

I was a *personal trainer*. Something about that title felt exciting. I was *something*. I dove in with determination and fire. The work was hard, but I was helping people transform, and it was transforming me too. I studied training theory and coaching techniques. People started calling me Ms. Motivator. I started making a good income. I was proud to tell family and friends what I was doing. I finally felt like I had found *my thing*.

I started dating a trainer I worked with. He was the kind of guy everyone loves—kind, loyal, and everyone's biggest cheerleader. His gym nickname was Mr. Motivator, so we were an easy match. We soon got engaged. We set a wedding date for the following New Year's Eve at my parents' home in Florida.

I became one of the top trainers at Crunch Fitness. My fiancé and I worked constantly and had only a couple of hours to be together between clients. I barely had time to call my mom or do my laundry or even work out myself. I didn't realize it at the time, but I was wading into another extreme: overworking to prove myself to everyone who thought I had failed at theater. I worked from 5:00 a.m. to 11:00 p.m. every day, including Sunday. Work became my priority over my faith. Because I was helping people and making a good income, I thought it was a worthy pursuit.

I had a career I was proud of, an apartment in a high-rise building on 61st and York, and a fiancé. But a nagging thought persisted: *I have everything I'm supposed to have in order to be happy, so why do I still feel empty?*

Have you ever reached the peak of a goal, what was supposed to be the *end* and realized there was still another mountain to climb? Describe what happened—and how you felt.

AND THEN WINDS AND RAIN CAME . . .

In early September my mom called to say that they were boarding up their house in Florida. Despite the strong warnings to evacuate, my parents decided to ride out this storm at home.

I watched the news at the gym as the storm rolled in. As it began to make landfall, the radar picture grew redder and redder—something I had never seen before.

My family's home was ravaged by Hurricane Ivan. My dad called the day after the hurricane, having waded through four miles of knee-high water and debris to get to a working phone at the police station. After hearing of the devastation, I knew my parents needed help. I talked to my fiancé, and we booked one-way tickets to Mobile, Alabama, the closest working airport.

We rented a truck and made the trek to my parents' home in Gulf Breeze. It was like driving through a war zone, with gutted houses, missing roofs, stray animals, and roaming residents. The closer we got to my house, the more my heart pounded. *What are we about to see?* As the familiar driveway came into sight, my breath left me.

The first floor was gone. A concrete stairwell from another house was in our backyard, and a neighbor's dinghy was sideways in our now-twisted palm trees. My mama's lush gardens were flattened and covered in debris. The sixteen-foot storm surge had left a ring of seaweed and sludge well above the second floor. My mom came out to meet us and, through her tears, all she could do was shrug, as if to say, *What do we do now?*

The new identity I had built as a top trainer in New York suddenly seemed insignificant. I told my fiancé we had to leave the city. There was no logic behind my decision—no jobs or places to live waiting for us in Florida—just an unshakable feeling I had to help my family. He agreed, so we left everything behind—clients, our apartment, even our furniture. Three weeks later we went to Florida with whatever we each could fit in a single suitcase.

JOY AMID THE RUINS

Despite the chaos, we never considered canceling the wedding. Our neighbors pitched in to make sure our house would be ready for the big day. We scrubbed seaweed-covered walls, moved tons of sand back to the beach, and reassembled toilets. We often showered outside in our bathing suits with the only working hose—jumping when water snakes would slither by.

When I wasn't prying rusty nails out of demolished doorways, I spent hours planning the wedding. I coped through creativity. I created the invitations, hand-painted our aisle runner, built our ceremony canopy, and sketched floral designs. Just as in the theater world I had known for most of my life, a love story could come alive through lighting, music, and these special pieces I created. My mom got me a copy of Preston Bailey's *Fantasy Weddings*, and I couldn't believe how he transformed mundane spaces—a warehouse, a stable, an aircraft hangar—into magical celebrations. I wanted to turn our ruins into a meaningful night of celebration too.

Somehow the house was ready just in time. My mom put the last doorknob on (backward, but there was no time to fix it) just ten minutes before the ceremony started in a tent on our driveway.

Our wedding was a celebration of hope and resilience. Friends from college sang, high school drama friends did readings, and my training mentor, Ray, was a groomsman. Even with our small town still in ruin, we escaped to joy as we danced the night away.

Yet something in my heart didn't feel completely whole. It had all happened so fast, and there had been so much pain and change in such a short time. My husband and I had gone from working 24-7, to a natural disaster, to this one celebratory night that seemed so good yet so disconnected from everything around it. I pushed those feelings aside as we flew to Montana for our honeymoon.

At negative thirty degrees, it wasn't the sparkling winter adventure we had hoped for. And I felt bad being on a honeymoon when there were still thousands in my community without homes. None of this felt right. I longed to go home— home to my family, but even more than that, I longed to find home in my soul.

I knew one thing: I loved designing and creating our wedding. I had fallen in love with the art of creating life-giving celebrations. Despite my love of training, this thought wouldn't escape me: *Maybe this is what I am supposed to do with my life.*

As you have been working through the pages of this book, what passions and dreams have been sparked in you? What "maybe" is on your heart?

I was willing to give "maybe" a chance. There were no smartphones back then, so I found a pay-per-use computer in the ski lodge lobby and paid ten dollars for ten minutes that changed my life. I searched the Internet for "how to start a business" and "how to buy a website." Four minutes in, I found a company that sold domain names. Six minutes in, I was scribbling potential company names on a hotel notepad. Nine minutes in, with my Internet time ticking down and pressuring me to move fast, I hit Purchase on BlissEventGroup.com. My event planning company was born.

This purchase of Internet real estate made me feel alive. You know that feeling when you just need to *go and do*? Despite being on our honeymoon, I was ready to go and do something that would give people hope and joy. Like right away. And I was tired of the bone-chilling cold. Neither of us was happy in Montana, so we left our honeymoon a week early.

CRUSHING NEWS

We arrived back in Florida and started thawing out. We were telling my parents about our short, chilly adventure when the phone rang. My mom answered, and her face went white at the news. Just hours later my mom and I were on a plane to Colorado to see my little brother, who had injured his spinal cord in a snowboarding accident. He had been taken into emergency surgery, and they didn't know if he would make it through the procedure.

Walking down the hallway of the intensive care unit, I felt the urgency of wanting to see Stephen as quickly as possible, coupled with an unspeakable fear that grew with every step. My brother loved mountain sports and was an avid rock climber and snowboarder. This was all taken from him in an instant when he snowboarded off a service road and cracked his spine.

Puffy from surgery, he didn't speak. He just looked at us with pain behind his eyes. His doctors were crowded around the foot of his bed when we walked in. They solemnly told us the news. "He will likely never walk again. There is a chance, but it would be a miracle."

WHY?

I prayed hard for my brother, but I wanted an audible voice to tell me he was going to be all right. I kept asking, *Why, God?* My mom and I were sad and angry at God—but trying not to show our negative emotions to anyone, especially to my brother.

You can imagine what happens when no one is feeling or talking: the strengths and weaknesses of relationships become transparent. In a few months, my fledgling marriage had been battered by more than it could withstand. But I couldn't talk to my mom about my marriage concerns because she was dealing with insurance claims and caring for her son. I couldn't reach out to my dad for comfort because he was struggling to maintain a business in a city that was in sudden financial ruin. My family teetered back and forth between caring for one another and fighting secret pain.

I have struggled more in writing this paragraph than any other in this book. This isn't pretty to type or remember, but it happened: my marriage crumbled. It happened so fast, like the hurricane that tore through our town. We lacked the firm foundation that only God can solidify. I remember the day I sat alone in the courthouse to finalize our divorce, less than a year after our wedding; and my dad telling me how disappointed he was; and my mom crying because her children's lives were falling apart before her eyes.

I know it was by my human failings, not God's hand, that my marriage fell apart. In sharing my failure and what followed, though, I hope it will help you know what I know now: your past and your mistakes—no matter how heavy or confusing or deep they run—do not define you. No matter what you have done or experienced, you can receive God's grace. His forgiveness is bigger than your mistakes. His power is bigger than your past or your present.

Because of God's grace, I no longer feel shame or guilt, but I have a lasting reminder of why I need God and His undeserved gift of forgiveness. Whether you've known Him for years or days—or perhaps this very moment is the first time you say, *Yes, Lord*—give it all to Him. Let go and let God. He will wipe your past away.

Making it happen means knowing God's GRACE is bigger than your mistakes.

TAKE ACTION

▶ Have you ever felt trapped by the shame and guilt of your past? Describe the mistakes of your past that you feel still define you. Then write out Psalm 103:12.

▶ Talk or write to God about a painful memory from your past. Yes, He knows all about our days and our pain, but He is there to talk things out with us to help us heal. He wants to turn our sorrow into joy. Read Matthew 11:28–30. Let it all go. If you are able to look back and see how God used that circumstance for good, take a moment to thank God for working through the pain. If you can't yet see His hand at work, ask God to comfort your heart with the truth that even though you may not know the *why*, you can always trust the *Who*.

▶ You are working so hard, friend. I am so proud of you for getting this far and doing the hard work. I have a little surprise gift for you. Go to www.LaraCasey.com /alittlesurprise.

PART TWO

TAKE THE LEAP

7

LEAP INTO TRUST

*When you are down to nothing,
God is up to something.*

At age twenty-six, I was living with my parents, unemployed, and divorced. This was not how my life was supposed to go. Everything felt shattered and lifeless.

I had been afraid to step back into the gym and face people from my hometown who knew about my failed marriage, but I needed a job to pay for my living expenses, getting my event planning company off the ground, and mounting debt from new therapy sessions. I confronted my fear and decided that life was too short to be afraid of what other people thought. I could either be held back by my fear of a few people making me feel small, or I could step back into the gym, help people, and start paying off my debt. So I took a job training people at the local gym.

One Sunday afternoon, a tall, handsome Navy gent walked up to me in the gym and introduced himself. I was doing cable crossovers—not the most flattering exercise—and had no makeup on, but he didn't flinch. With a hint of playfulness he said, "Hi, is your name pronounced Lah-rah or Laura?" I laughed at his attempt at a pickup line, thinking, *Here I am, newly divorced, living at home, and struggling under a mountain of debt—this guy has no idea what he is getting into! Good luck getting a date out of me, mister!*

Just days later, however, I ate both my words and dinner with Ari. I don't remember what we ate, but I remember what I said. I wasted no time making sure he wasn't wasting his time. As the waiter poured our waters, I laid all my baggage on our crisp, white linen tablecloth. Divorce, family tragedy, depression, therapy, debt—all of it. I waited for Ari to excuse himself for a Navy emergency, but that didn't happen. Instead, he nodded and smiled and said, "Well, here's where I am in life . . ." He told me about his family challenges, his failed dating experiences, and his unexpected path with the Navy. Ari made me feel accepted—not despite my flaws but *with* them.

I certainly wasn't looking for love. After all I had been through that year, dating was the furthest thing from my mind. I had accepted the idea that I might never marry again. But sometimes God shakes things up to get us to step into His plans—plans that are far better than ours.

Have you ever had to "eat your words" as a result of God shaking up your plans? Describe what happened.

FAITH OR FEELINGS?

Bringing Ari to my house for the first time was humbling. My French chef mama, overwhelmed by all the recent tragedies in our family, had stopped cooking. The once-joyful sound of her voice wafting through the kitchen gave way to the screech of Styrofoam at our table. My quiet dad poured the water. My brother, living at home, came to the table in his wheelchair. The heaviness settled in at the table as we waited to see if Ari would leave. But just as at our first dinner together, Ari didn't judge us. He smiled and said, "So, Dr. Casey, Lara tells me you were a flight surgeon too."

Ari joined us for dinner more often, and laughter returned to our dinner table. My mom got back in the kitchen and looked forward to this appreciative Navy gent's healthy appetite. My dad looked forward to reminiscing about his military days and hearing about Ari's flight surgery training. And then there was my brother. My parents and I didn't know how to talk to him about what happened, but Ari knew that ailing people can feel alienated when their sicknesses are ignored. So Ari kept asking Stephen how he was doing even if the response was just a nod.

Weeks later, the impossible happened. My brother took a step. He proved his doctors wrong and began to WALK. As I type, he is in Colorado, snowboarding the same path on which he was injured over a decade ago. We had all prayed hard for him, but there was so much heaviness in those days that it was hard to believe God was listening. We had lost hope on so many levels, but hope was taking steps right before our eyes.

Stephen's steps made me believe that anything was possible. God *was* listening in our brokenness. Even though we couldn't feel it, He was listening, healing muscle fibers and broken courage. His steps gave me courage to open my heart to new possibilities.

I started to feel butterflies, like sparkles in my soul, whenever Ari was around. But it was far too soon. My counselor had urged me to wait at least two years before considering another relationship so I could have time to heal. *But he's so kind,* I reasoned. *He doesn't care about my past. And he is so handsome.*

I knew I had gone to extremes to get things I wanted in the past, and I didn't want to fall into that trap again. *No, no, no! It's too soon,* I told myself. *But maybe this happened for a reason. Maybe Ari is what's missing from my life.* I was just starting to heal from my broken marriage—and now I was falling for this guy from the gym? *I know I shouldn't . . . but it just feels right.*

Are we supposed to follow our feelings?

True or false: "Follow your heart" is a verse from the Bible.

> **False.** *God doesn't want us to follow our feelings; He wants us to be still with our feelings and see if they align with His heart. If they don't, they can lead us astray.*

Before you make any big decisions, ask yourself this question: "Am I acting on faith or feelings?"

When it comes to our faith, we must choose trust over feelings. There are many times we cannot *feel* God working, but we can trust that He is. We may not *feel* loved by God, but we can trust that His love never changes.

Feelings aren't the enemy, though; they are opportunities to draw closer to God and learn His wisdom. The more we come to God with our feelings and ask, "What do I do with this?" the more He brings our emotions in line with His heart. And the more we align our hearts with His, the bigger our faith becomes, leading us to be able to take bold leaps forward without fear.

A leap of trust doesn't mean haphazardly throwing everything to the wind. A leap of trust means that you consider your feelings, align them with God's heart, and then leap, trusting that He will catch you.

When God says go, then *go*. Trust that He has a really good plan.

Check yourself with God. What leaps are you considering? Are they born of faith or feelings?

If you're not sure, then take time to talk to God about it. He will give you answers in His timing. Remember: ripening can happen in our times of waiting.

Ari and I began dating. It was still so soon after my wedding and divorce that often, when we were out at dinner, friends who had missed the wedding would approach us and excitedly greet my "new husband." These awkward greetings didn't faze Ari, though, further showing me that there was something radically different about this guy's heart.

Ari was my opposite in many ways. I was the creative dreamer, and he was the logical doctor, like my dad. I was excitable, reactionary, and a people pleaser, and he was focused, unshakable, and brutally honest. I loved color and glitter paint, and he really didn't like glitter paint. His idea of hell on earth was going into my favorite place—a Michael's craft store. But sometimes opposites attract because they balance each other out.

At a Greek restaurant near my house, Ari said he had

something to tell me. I figured it couldn't be as bad as anything I had shared with him about my life, so I ate my hummus platter and listened cheerfully. "I know it's early in our relationship to be talking about this, but you should know that I have to marry a Jewish girl," he explained.

Using the shreds of acting skill left behind from my CMU days, I tried to appear as though this enormous statement didn't affect me. "Okay, um, thanks for telling me," I forced out. "We've only been dating for two months, though. We can talk about that later, if we get serious."

But we *were* getting serious. And his time at the base was short, putting pressure on our relationship to be defined—he was only in Florida for another four months. We went on romantic dates and had long conversations about life. My family was in love with him. I was in love with him, too, I realized. *How could You put a guy like this in my life, Lord, and then make it impossible for us to be together?*

Not giving God a chance to answer, I came up with my own plan: *I'll just sweep him off his feet so he'll forget about this "marrying a Jewish girl" thing. I can control this!*

Rather than listening to God, I told myself I had all the answers.

I was going to *fix this.*

"CHAMELEONING"

My unchecked feelings gave way to what I call "chameleoning." Chameleons see their surroundings and, to avoid potential threats, change their bodies to blend in. I feared that if I didn't change myself, I might lose Ari. So I asked Ari about Jewish culture and customs. I went to temple with him one Saturday. They were starting a Judaism 101 class, and he suggested we attend so I could learn more about his faith.

Have you ever found yourself "chameleoning"? Have you felt compelled to change—or to hide part of who you are—in order to please someone?

How did that make you feel? How did the situation turn out?

The first class was fun. Twenty of us, mostly couples, ate matzo ball soup and sang songs in Hebrew. I tried to pronounce *challah* without spitting on anyone. I imagined Jesus doing the things the rabbi was teaching us about: celebrating Passover, learning the Torah, and going to the temple with His family. I hadn't read much of the Old Testament, but I started to get a cultural picture of the life Jesus lived.

The second class, however, dropped a bomb in my lap. As the rabbi explained the steps to conversion, he read this: "You will be asked to renounce your former faith." As we drove home that night, I was silent. The thought of renouncing my faith in Jesus made me sick. I had turned away from Him countless times and wavered in my obedience, but I also knew in my heart that He was always there.

"Ari, I don't know how to tell you this," I finally told him. "I will go to temple with you, and I want to learn more about your faith, but I can't *not* believe in Jesus." Double negatives aside, I knew my words were true and right.

Have you ever had to choose between your faith and your relationship with someone? What did you choose? Why?

If you could go back and make that choice again, would you do anything differently?

Neither of us remembers Ari's reaction. Our feelings of being in love clouded all logic.

"I DO," AGAIN

The date of Ari's next move grew closer. He was assigned to Port Hueneme in California, worlds away from my home in Florida. That New Year's Eve, at the stroke of midnight, Ari asked me to move to California with him. The confetti was fluttering around us, and people were celebrating, and it felt magical. I said yes.

One week later, as he was plotting our drive from Pensacola to Los Angeles, he said casually—still looking at the computer screen—"So what do you think about getting married in Vegas on the way to California?" I laughed, assuming he was joking. He turned to me with a boyish, hopeful grin. He was serious.

But I'm not Jewish, and we've only been together four months. But Vegas—that's crazy! My parents will flip out. Did you just propose to me staring at a computer screen?

Ari told me all the "logical" reasons we should get married. Most important, with the Iraq war rumbling, there was a good chance he would be deployed, and if we weren't married, I wouldn't be able to go on base or know where he was on

74

deployment. "Many military couples have small ceremonies to make it legal," he said, "and then bigger 'real' weddings later. We don't have to tell anyone yet, and when our families are okay with us getting married, we'll have a real wedding." He somehow won me over. I told him I would agree . . . but only after he redid this far-too-casual proposal and got down on one knee.

I was a mess the night before the wedding. I kept thinking, *I want to marry him, but I'm scared to fail again. I'm afraid of our faiths not matching. Will our parents ever be happy about our marriage? Are we making a mistake? This is crazy.*

Ari assured me everything would be fine. There was something about his steadfast calm that made me believe it was, in fact, all going to be all right. Five months after our first meeting in the gym, I took a leap and said "I do" again.

PLAYING HOUSE

Eloping in Vegas felt like the start of a wildly romantic adventure. Keeping the secret was fun at first. There was no one to check in on how our marriage was going, no registry gifts to put away, no fancy wedding to talk about—it was just us. Married. In love. Playing house together. It was freeing to be away from Florida, where so much turmoil had happened. No one but Ari knew me in California. I could truly start fresh.

I renewed my personal training certification, unpacked my paints, and cracked open a wedding magazine that listed the top wedding planners across the United States. My fledgling event planning company was in the hands of a new business partner back in Florida, so I decided to apply for my dream wedding jobs ia. I circled the names of all the people I wanted to ...k ror and decided I had nothing to lose by trying, and trying hard. I took the leap and e-mailed them all, telling them about my passion for creating transformative celebrations. I figured the worst thing people could say was no, but the possibility that they could say yes just might change everything. Even if they did say no, I would keep trying. I would keep creating. Our purpose cannot depend on someone else's yes. The only yes that matters is God's.

Have you ever avoided taking a risk because you were afraid of someone saying no? Are you putting off taking a leap right now because of your fear of someone saying no?

Read aloud the following statement several times, until it seeps in to your mind and heart:

My purpose cannot depend on someone else's yes.
The only yes that matters is God's.

A living-room dance party ensued when I learned I had been offered jobs at not one but *two* prestigious event design companies. I was flabbergasted. I had taken a giant leap and landed smack in the center of an exciting new path.

I was like a kid in a candy store, surrounded by the best in events. Though my jobs regularly involved meetings with celebrity clients, I was in awe not of the A-listers but of the creativity around me. I worked an event where they installed a dozen giant magnolia trees around the dance floor—I couldn't believe you could do that with flowers and lighting. I kept thinking, *There's more to weddings than stuffed chicken and tulle! I want to tell everyone in the South about this!*

Life at home proved less exciting as the fun of our secret elopement dissipated. Ari's parents lived an hour away, and we were paranoid they would find out about our marriage. Maybe a Navy friend would slip and say something, or I would forget to take off my ring before having dinner at their house. We felt guilty, wondering when we would be able to come clean to them.

The facts we had pushed under the table during our fast-and-furious courtship began clawing at us. Ari got angry when I read my Bible, and the tension mounted. The first year of our marriage was one of fighting, yelling, tears, and slammed doors. He resented me for not converting to Judaism, and I resented him for not accepting my faith. Many fights would end in, "We shouldn't have gotten married."

Right before our one-year wedding anniversary, Ari came home from work early. My unshakable husband cried as he told me he had been given deployment orders to Iraq. He was to leave in sixteen days. "I called your parents on the way home and told them we're married," he added. He had called his parents to tell them the news too. My heart sank.

Months of guilt and shame poured out with my tears. I had taken a leap when I said "I do." But now I was starting to question my decision. With my marriage lying in ruins amid our secrets, anger, and now physical separation, was there any hope that God could save it?

I was about to learn something life-changing: *following God doesn't mean the path will be easy; it means it will be meaningful.* When we choose to follow Him, we can trust He has a very good plan for our lives—and here's the key—He can change *anything.*

Making it happen means trusting that God can change ANYTHING.

TAKE ACTION

▶ What in your life feels like it has been crumbling? What change feels impossible? Write it out.

▶ Write the following verse on a bright-colored sticky note or notecard and place it where you can read it every day:

> Trust in the LORD with all your heart
>   and lean not on your own understanding;
> in all your ways submit to him,
>   and he will make your paths straight. (Prov. 3:5–6)

Now personalize this verse, speaking it aloud as a prayer of trust: "Lord, I trust You with all my heart. I will not lean on my own understanding, but in all my ways I will submit to You. And You will make my paths straight. Amen." Believe those words, friend. God is God, and He will show you the way.

8

TAKE A LEAP OF FAITH

Sometimes the only possible NEXT STEP is to take a bold LEAP OF FAITH.

left my glamorous jobs and moved back in with my parents while Ari was in Iraq. Despite the pain of our first year of marriage, my love and respect for him multiplied during his deployment. My husband was at war—a war he might never return from. I worried about him constantly. I waited by my phone to hear from him on days he could call me from his clinic. If I didn't hear from him for long periods, I knew the base was under threat. It was terrifying. I stopped watching the news to avoid the names of fallen soldiers running in a banner across the bottom of the screen. I didn't tell Ari for fear I would upset him, but I prayed for him often. I prayed for his safety and that this experience would open his heart to me and to God.

At the same time, being away from the acute pain of our marriage, I felt *free*. I could be myself without fear of a fight. I could read the Bible. I could talk about God. I went to church every Sunday, and my mom even started coming with me. I played my Christian music loudly, dove in to designing weddings with my own company again, and drenched canvases in glitter paint, pouring sparkling pigment on my dimmed soul. *How many holes in my heart can I fill in seven months?*

Immersed in my clients' weddings and desperate to keep my mind off bomb threats, I often found myself dreaming of pretty things. Then one night I found myself on my thirteen-inch PC, mocking up a wedding magazine cover.

The next night, I played with it again.

The next night, I started to dream up photo shoots.

The next night, I looked up domain names.

The next night, I decided I was nuts, but I e-mailed some friends about doing a photo shoot. They thought I was nuts too.

The thought of creating beauty in a world that felt so heavy with war and despair—and breathing life into my own—kept me coming back to that thirteen-inch screen night after night.

But this felt so much bigger than me. *A magazine? Me? I don't have a degree in journalism or publishing. I don't have any idea what I'm doing. But . . . there seems to be something to this.*

My creative passions were set swirling by the possibility of this someday magazine housing them all. In these pages I could be an artist, designer, and encourager, using all the gifts God had given me. I imagined putting the magazine in grocery stores and churches—maybe even at bridal shows. It didn't matter where we put it, though, as long as it existed.

Sometimes the only possible next step is to take a bold leap of faith.

What bold leaps of faith have you taken in the past? How did those leaps change your life? How did your leaps of faith help you to live on purpose?

Perhaps you feel like you've never taken a leap of faith before. Welcome to your new beginning. What leaps of faith are you considering taking now?

Leaps of faith come in all shapes and sizes. Your next leap might be moving somewhere new or quitting your job. It might be ending a dating relationship that is not ultimately leading you closer to God. It might be putting yourself out there and using your creative talents. And this is the key, as we learned in the previous chapter: when you are taking a leap of faith—to God— you can trust that He will be there to catch you.

The biggest leap in dance is the grand jeté, and it's much like the biggest leaps in our lives: you take to the air with powerful, springing force and extend your whole being into an expansive, gliding split. It's terrifying and exhilarating all at the same time. It feels like flying, as if you might never land. But you build wings on the way down, preparing you for the next leap—because there will be many ahead. A frame of my life flashed before me: my college ballet teacher, Judy, yelling, "Jeté, jeté, jeté!" as we dashed across the resin-speckled studio. As I sat at the computer, I heard God whisper to my heart, *Grand jeté, Lara Casey!*

I had no clue what I was doing. I didn't know the first thing about organizing, writing, or designing a magazine. I loved playing around with Microsoft Publisher, but I had no idea what *signatures*, *bleed*, or *CMYK* meant. When God wants us to make something happen, though, He gives us exactly what we need. He kept bringing me back to my laptop, searching the Internet for guidance and creating something out of what felt like nothing.

And there was a bigger picture in all this. In my search for how to have a stronger marriage, I had read Gary Chapman's *The Five Love Languages*. Ari and I were definitely speaking different love languages, and Gary's advice was eye-opening. Gary described exactly what had happened to us:

> Being in love is an emotional and obsessive experience. However, emotions change and obsessions fade. Research indicates that the average life span of the "in love" obsession is two years. For some it may last a bit longer; for some, a bit less. Then we come down off the emotional high and those aspects of life that we disregarded in our euphoria begin to become important. Our differences begin to emerge and we often find ourselves arguing with the person whom we once thought to be perfect. We have now discovered for ourselves that being in love is not the foundation for a happy marriage. Before marriage, we are carried along by the force of the in-love obsession. After marriage, we revert to being the people we were before we "fell in love." True love cannot begin until the "in love" experience has run its course.[1]

Ari and I had been deeply "in love," and it had run its course. As I saw our challenges through a new lens, my hope grew that we could work them out when he returned. *Couples should learn this stuff before they get married*, I thought. *Maybe I could help strengthen their relationships by putting it in this magazine.* I found Gary's e-mail address on his website and e-mailed to ask if he would be willing to do an interview for our first issue. To my surprise and delight, he said yes.

I had one rule as I continued to create the magazine, something I had learned from getting my jobs in California: it never hurts to ask. So I did. *Big Name Wedding Photographer, can you send me your best wedding photos to put in our magazine that doesn't exist yet? Famous Author, can I interview you? And have signed copies of your books to give away to readers? Magazine Wholesaler Person, I just started a small magazine out of my childhood bedroom. I have zero experience, but I have more passion than a hen has feathers. Could you help me get that bar-code thingy on the front?* That's not exactly how the conversations went, but it's pretty close. I am "Google and ask a lot of dumb questions" taught.

I also wrote a blog to try to inspire brides. I wanted to show Southern brides all that I had seen and experienced in Los Angeles, and it caught on. Readers and wedding professionals were excited to see something new in the South, and I was excited to be a part of a creative community. The blog gained popularity, and just as we printed our first issue, paid for with my tiny life savings, Ari came home safely from Iraq.

As we drove from his training station in Arizona back to California, I cautiously suggested we listen to *The Five Love Languages* audiobook. I worried Ari might be offended by the references to Christianity, but instead we laughed and talked about what we had been through. I felt a flicker of hope.

We had only a few months left in California before Ari was scheduled to begin his radiology residency at the University of North Carolina in Chapel Hill. I used that time to take another leap of faith: I sent a letter to Curtis Circulation asking them to consider signing us. Curtis was the company that helped all the big magazines get on newsstands, and they decided to take a chance on us. *Yes! We are going to be on newsstands all over the United States! I have no idea what I'm doing, and the biggest circulation agent said yes!*

I bought some business cards online, gave myself the title *editor-in-chief*, and Googled like crazy to learn how to apply for a trademark on the magazine name. I filed my trademark paperwork and told everyone who would listen that the magazine was going to be at Barnes & Noble.

With Ari's military commitment complete, we packed our bags to move to the South. Things were looking up. My parents were proud, my husband was back from war, and I had a popular wedding blog and a hot new magazine about to be shipped to newsstands.

THE SMALLEST FISH IN THE POND

Just as the movers took my desk out from under me on our moving day, my event-planning-company business partner called to tell me that she had been put on bed rest. We had sixteen weddings on the books and only the two of us to execute them—and now I was going to be in North Carolina, not Florida. *What am I going to do about these weddings?*

As the panic set in, not even ten minutes later, my mom called to tell me a cease and desist letter had arrived at their house in Florida. The letter stated that the name of my magazine was too similar to something their client, a well-known company, had trademarked. Within a matter of minutes I was smacked with two enormous business roadblocks before we had even hit newsstands. I broke down and sobbed on the floor as the movers continued to take our belongings out to the truck. One mover guy even stepped over me to grab a lamp.

I didn't have a lawyer. I had never even heard of a cease and desist letter. I was the smallest fish in the pond, and I couldn't understand why a giant magazine was coming after me. As I saw it, my options were to fight it and lose with money I didn't have, or not fight it and lose anyway. So I did what any new kid on the block would do. I wiped away my tears, picked up a pen, and wrote the scary lawyers a really nice letter. I kindly asked them not to make me pull the copies I had funded with my life savings. "I'm just a girl with a dream," I wrote, "working from my tiny apartment. If you just let me put these copies out, I promise I'll change the name of the magazine the next time around. I've put everything I have into this magazine, and so many people are relying on me to make this happen. I don't have the money for a lawyer, and I want this with all of my heart." I asked, and the scary lawyers ate me up for that sugar-sweet letter. They sued me for it, as an admission of guilt.

My life was spontaneously combusting. I had no idea what to do or feel at that point. Was I supposed to do something else with my life? I had gone through three major career changes in five years. How was I supposed to start over—yet again—with nothing? How was I going to break the news to all our readers and vendors who believed in us and were expecting a magazine on shelves any day? How was I going to tell my parents that I had failed yet again?

Many times, when we make a great effort and see some progress, only to have something fall apart, we get discouraged and want to quit altogether.

Have you ever felt that way? Like a million times? Me too. On the road to making it happen, you will encounter countless

You are going to fail sometimes, and things won't always go the way you hoped. But here's the beautiful paradox about failure: *failure will get you further than fear.* Failure has the potential to guide us to be better, to summon our strength, and to push forward with greater determination.

What pitfalls have you encountered so far in your journey? In what ways do you feel that you have failed or circumstances have not gone as you had hoped?

If you are tempted to despair during these times, remember this freeing truth: *you will learn more from your failures than you will learn from any of your successes.* Our failures are gifts, allowing us to learn, grow, redirect, and take new—and potentially better—paths.

It sure seemed as if God wanted me to go in a different direction with all these roadblocks I was encountering—I felt I had only a tiny glimmer left of my once-grand vision. But sometimes a spark is all it takes to start a fire.

BEGINNING AGAIN—AGAIN

The path ahead was anything but cake. The stress of our move and my legal issues strained our marriage. Ari and I arrived in North Carolina with just an air mattress and some clothes. If you know anything about military moves, you know it took an eternity to get our stuff to Chapel Hill. Ari left our bare apartment every morning to learn how to live as a civilian and a resident, and I put the pieces of what I had built back together.

I sat on that air mattress, got on Craigslist, and put out a plea for interns to help me run the blog and magazine. I hunted for a new lawyer. Using money from Ari's first paycheck that had been earmarked for furniture, I applied for a new trademark, this time on the name *Southern Weddings*. My new lawyer assured me this trademark was a shoo-in. I cautiously started over. To my surprise and great relief, advertisers trickled in. We went to press with a new name, a new design, and a fresh outlook.

As I watched the copies come off the press, my phone rang. It was my lawyer. "Lara, the trademark has been rejected. I'm so sorry. There's nothing we can do."

I felt a passion boil inside of me. Deciding to take a bold leap of faith, I told my lawyer, "We *can't* start over again. Fix this. Appeal it. I don't care what the government says. Fix it!"

After a long pause, he said, "Um, I'll try." We appealed the decision and kept moving.

The first issue debuted to rave reviews, and we sold out in three months. Readers were delighted. Sponsors were thrilled. Our distribution agents were elated. But I was scared. The success of the magazine was bittersweet. The more popular it got, the more scared I became. It takes weeks, sometimes months to get correspondence back on a trademark appeal. I felt like an open target. I kept thinking that any day I would get another letter from scary lawyers who wanted to crush my dreams.

The day we sold the last box of magazines, I received an e-mail from my lawyer. I was conditioned to cringe every time I saw his name pop up in my inbox, but this time my cringe turned to tears—grateful, happy tears. Our trademark had been approved. I cried at my desk before shouting my joy to the rooftops and to just about anyone whose number I had in my phone. Finally, finally, *finally!*

My joy wasn't really about a trademark or a piece of paper, though. It was about losing what I thought was everything more times than I can count, failing over and over and over again, and then getting back up.

Our most grand leaps—the ones that change everything—come from first being knocked down. It's in the depths of our challenges, when we are left with what feels like nothing, that we can sometimes see more clearly. All the fluff stripped away, we see what matters. Life doesn't have to be perfect for you to take that grand leap of faith. Your circumstances don't have to be just right. Leaping is the act of taking the risk to propel yourself from one place—gliding above and through the past challenges—to somewhere better.

Leap into the air with abandon, friend. The best is yet to come.

Making it happen means taking a bold LEAP OF FAITH.

TAKE ACTION

▶ What leap of faith are you considering now? Write it out in bold letters. Be specific. And it wouldn't be a leap of faith if it wasn't a little (or a lot) scary to write it out. You can do this!

▶ In Matthew 7:7, Jesus told us, "Ask and it will be given to you; seek and you will find; knock and the door will be opened to you." *Ask. Seek. Knock.* Whatever leap of faith has been on your heart, ask God for it. Then, wait on His reply and, whether it is a yes or a no, trust in His perfect plan.

9

LEAP INTO WHAT MATTERS

Stop the glorification of BUSY.

The light flashed green on my dreams, so I pressed my foot on the gas pedal as hard as I could. I said yes to *everything*. I took every speaking engagement, every interview, and every travel request. I turned the master bedroom in our tiny apartment into the *Southern Weddings* office so I could accommodate three new employees and two interns. I worked late nights and was glued to social media to try to network and grow. People asked me for business advice, so I started a consulting company too. I continued to plan weddings with my event planning company, traveling between states for meetings and wedding days. I didn't dare say no to anything, in case I might miss an opportunity.

A magazine, a blog, a wedding production company, a

consulting company, speaking engagements, conferences—I was like a freight train . . . full speed ahead. I was speeding so fast toward success that I couldn't see what I was demolishing on the way. I thought I was doing the right thing: grow, grow, *grow*. I didn't see the crash coming.

What does *successful* look like to you? What do you believe you need to do in order to *get ahead*?

Ari and I became roommates. We never saw each other, and when we did, I'd be working and he'd be disconnected, lost in video games or TV. We spent our days searching for fulfillment in all the wrong places. I built friendships with popular people and did whatever I could to win their approval, including flirting with guys on my travels. They made me feel beautiful and sought-after, a stark contrast to what I was feeling at home. I escaped to my growing magazine and to relationships that distracted me from what mattered. Ari escaped to work and late nights with friends.

Our relationship began to feel beyond repair again. We fought constantly, as we had in our first year of marriage. We slept in separate beds. I shoved my faith aside in favor of work, and Ari declared that he didn't believe in God anymore. I worked nineteen-hour days, seven days a week, chasing the uncatchable once again.

It's so easy to get off track. The world's standard of perfect tries to lure us in at every turn. The world makes a lot of promises: If you are perfect, you will be happy. If you have money, you will be happy. If you have fame, you will be happy. If you aren't the best, you will be a failure. If you aren't the best, you will *be nothing.* Well, friends, the world is a liar. I was miserable. I was moving at the speed of light, driven by fear instead of God.

I talked about how busy I was all the time, like it was a badge of honor, as if *busy* equaled *successful.* Well, I was successful, all right: I was a pro at covering the bags under my eyes with tons of makeup. I was stellar at feeding my ego to try to bandage my shattered soul. I was an expert excuse-maker, quick to reply to invitations from friends with, "I have to work." I was so good at being in control that God couldn't get a word in edgewise. I was great at living a happy life online so I could escape from the turmoil in my crumbling marriage.

Have you ever believed any of the world's lies about success? Read the list below and circle the lies you have believed:

- If you are perfect, you will be successful.
- If you have money, you will be happy.
- If you have fame, you will be loved.
- If you aren't the best, you will be a failure.
- If you aren't the best, you will be *nothing.*

What does God's Word say in contrast to these lies? For starters, read Psalm 119:35: "Make me walk along the path of your commands, for that is where my happiness is found" (NLT).

BUT GOD . . .

Out of the blue, a friend sent me an e-mail telling me that my fast-paced life was "going nowhere." He told me that God wanted my marriage with Ari to be put back together. He said he didn't care if I hated him for this e-mail; he had to tell me the truth.

I fumed, thinking, *How dare he say this to me!* I cried and resisted the urge to punch things. I was angry because what he'd said was true, and I feared the truth. God was speaking to me in those pixels on the screen: *You are living a sinful life and going nowhere, fast. I want your marriage with Ari to be healed. Kick and scream all you want, but Lara . . . I am the truth and the way and the life.*

It was Saturday. I had just finished a long two weeks of travel, during which my employees told me they were disappointed in me for a laundry list of things. I was afraid to face them on Monday, for fear they would all quit.

My mom had just called to tell me she didn't like a photo she had seen of me having drinks with people on my travels. I hung up on her.

My bank accounts had dwindled to next to nothing, thanks to my extravagant travels and frivolous spending. I wasn't sure how I was going to make my next payment on the flashy car I couldn't afford but felt like I *needed.*

I didn't know where Ari was that weekend. I assumed he went out of town, maybe.

And this ridiculous e-mail lingered in my inbox.

Everything was crashing in, and I felt like I was powerless to change it.

But God . . .

But God isn't a God of logic. He is *God.*

God doesn't care about the mistakes you've made in the past. He wants your heart.

Read those two sentences again, this time out loud. Do you believe that, friend? I didn't. If I had read my own book a few years ago, I would have said a firm and resounding, "Yeah, right!" If that's you, stay with me. I wrote this book for you.

A PLACE TO FEEL LOVED

There was a church near our house that was always bustling with people—not just on Sundays but on most days of the week. I would see kids and families happily pouring out of the building as I passed them on my way to Target or the airport. I hadn't been to church since Ari's deployment almost two years earlier. *I am too busy for church*, I thought. *I am making things happen.* Church could wait.

That Sunday morning, though, on the way to Target to buy something I didn't need, I made a sharp turn into the church parking lot. Like a thirsty animal desperate for water, I walked in and sat down in the back.

It was clear to me, after a few minutes, that this diverse group of people all knew each other really well. I could sense their genuine love for one another. Suddenly I felt paranoid, exposed. *What if these people ask me about my life? All of these people seem so nice and good, and I'm a mess.*

I felt a hand on my shoulder and turned around to see a jolly older man smiling at me. "Hi! I'm Bob!" he said. He gave me a bear hug and asked me how I was doing, as if he had known me for years. Then a kind-looking blonde woman came up and gave me a hug before even introducing herself. "This is Jan," Bob said with a laugh.

"Hello," Jan said. "We're so grateful you are here. Can I sit next to you?" *Well, this isn't going to be the private church experience I had hoped for, where I just slip in and slip out after.*

I left the building that morning and felt good. Bob and Jan and the other people I met didn't want to know what I did for a living. They didn't even ask. They just wanted to be with me and make me feel loved. No pressure. Just love.

There was something different about these people. Whatever it was, I wanted to feel it more often. I went back on Wednesday night for a marriage class that Jan's husband, Mitch, was teaching. I wanted my marriage with Ari to be put back together. I wanted to know the truth, the way, and how to finally get a life.

THE IMPOSSIBLE IS POSSIBLE

I expected a class where we would talk about what the Bible says about marriage and how we all needed to do more of that, the end, amen. Instead, Mitch asked us about the challenges we were facing in marriage. These people weren't afraid to be honest: couple after couple shared their very intimate struggles. These people were the real deal—they were like family. My hand gravitated upward while my brain screamed, *No! Don't share! These people will judge you!*

But God kept nudging me to step out in faith and just *say it.* Stepping out in faith has to potentially cost you something—in my case, what these nice people thought of me. Sometimes you have to lose where you are to get somewhere better.

I didn't want to face the truth about my life myself, much less let other people know how broken I was. But the risk of letting others in was worth the possibility of positive change.

"Hi. I'm Lara," I said. "I'm new here, but I have to tell you that ly inspired and encouraged by all of your stories." I felt the tears well up. "I've been married to Ari for five years. He doesn't believe in God. I want our marriage to be better, but I don't know what to do."

Mitch smiled and said tenderly, "All things are possible with God."

I glanced around and saw everyone looking back at me. I had feared judgment in their eyes, but they were smiling too. They knew firsthand what I didn't yet. *With God, the impossible is possible.*

In that room that night, I heard a whisper of freedom: the absence of shame.

They offered encouragement, telling me they would pray for us. They invited me over for dinner. They asked for my phone number. I was hesitant, but it's hard to say no to people who really want to know you, not get something from you. I could feel the care these people had for one another. They were honest and humble. They didn't judge me. They made me feel hope.

Why are they like this? What makes them so content, even though many are struggling with cancer, unemployment, loss, and finances? Is this what knowing Jesus does? It felt so radical to me. They made me feel valued just as I was, in the midst of my brokenness, not because of my accomplishments. They didn't care about how many followers I had on social media; they cared about my heart.

THE MACHINE

But *I* still cared about how many followers I had on social media. Life didn't magically change overnight. I began spending a combined 2 hours at church and at the marriage class each week, but for the other 166 hours, I was still lost in the machine. The Internet and my businesses spun on at lightning speed. I had one toe in God's world, but the rest of me was keeping that machine running. I knew it had to slow down more, but I didn't know how.

I'll never forget the day I stepped out of church to answer a client's call. The joyful sound of the choir singing wafted through the hallway as I hurried out to answer. "Wait. Are you at church?" my client asked me. My body was there, all right, but my heart and mind were elsewhere. This was my phone call from God, saying, *Lara, wake up!* I may have been in the building, but I was still putting my exhausting rat race before the one thing that could bring me true success and joy.

Busy is the enemy of peace. Busy takes us away from our purpose. Busy is not truly productive in the big picture. Busy means life's joys and surprises can't find a way into our lives because we're moving too fast to see and experience them. I don't know about you, but I don't want to move so fast that I miss my life.

Read this question very slowly to let it marinate in your heart: *Are you striving to keep your machine running?*

Can you imagine living the way you are now, with no time, peace, or rest, for another year? Or even another day? What would happen if you put on the brakes and stopped the machine?

I was afraid to put on the brakes and be free to spend time with Ari because I didn't want to get into a shouting match. I want to face the pain and emptiness in our lives. In my frustration and desire for radical change, part of me wanted to just move my furniture around (I think I did do that) or get a new haircut (I did that too) to try to make life better. Part of me wanted to fold my business and escape. Dealing with what really needed change felt too overwhelming.

Sometimes our lives are like a tangled necklace chain. We want to shake it and pull it a couple of times to make it straight again, but it needs careful, thoughtful unraveling. What needs thoughtful unraveling in your life?

In his book *Love Does*, Bob Goff said this about success: "I used to be afraid of failing at something that really mattered to me, but now I'm more afraid of succeeding at things that don't matter."[1]

Though I had stepped back into church and deeply desired change, I still struggled hard with glorifying busyness. I thought I could still do things my way and somehow grow closer with God at the same time. But my ways weren't working. Scratch that—my ways were working *too much*. My desire for success had taken over, driving me to the point of nearly losing it all. I was succeeding at what didn't matter. Something big had to change—fast.

Making it happen means succeeding in what Matters.

TAKE ACTION

► Are you moving so fast that you feel like you are missing your life? Get out a piece of paper—or your journal—and write out everything you plan to do in the next twenty-four hours. Be very specific: include small tasks like "wake up," "take a shower," or "answer e-mails"—as well as bigger things like "finish a work project," or "eat dinner with my family." Include the time you might spend on distractions such as social media or TV.

► Now look over your list. What can you cross out to stay focused on what really matters? What steps can you take to add to—or take away from—your list? Examples: put a sticky note on your computer that says, "Focus on what matters"; ask a friend to be your Make It Happen accountability partner and tell her about what distracts you (and ask her the same so you can encourage each other); unplug or turn off your Internet for a while to work on a project; or simply cross off the things on your list that could be replaced with intentional living. Sometimes the simple act of making a written commitment—something we can see—helps us to make it happen. Focus on what matters, and forget the rest.

PART THREE

LIVE ON PURPOSE

10

FOLLOW THE REAL
SUCCESS EQUATION

The goal of life isn't to make a lot of money. It's to make a life that MEANS SOMETHING.

Mathematically speaking, it seems logical that working more hours means more productivity. So working fourteen-hour days to *get ahead* and never taking a weekend off so you can make it happen would mean you would be making more money too. The equation would be: More Time Spent Working + Some More Work = More Productivity, More Money, and, therefore, More Happiness. Right?

Work itself is not a bad thing. The Bible even tells us that we are supposed to work hard for what matters: "Whatever you do, work heartily, as for the Lord and not for men" (Col. 3:23 ESV). Whatever you do—whether cleaning the house, designing

s, changing diapers, or petitioning Congress—work
...,.. love this word! *Heartily* means with sincerity, zest, or
gusto. God desires us to work wholeheartedly, giving even the
mundane tasks of life meaning by giving them purpose.

When we work heartily for the Lord, the mundane becomes
meaningful, and the bigger tasks are given greater energy and
focus. For instance, creating an issue of *Southern Weddings* is
more important to me now than in our early years. We want
couples to have marriages more beautiful than their weddings.
When the purpose for your work is aimed at God's heart, it
makes you want to work a whole lot harder. The payoff for us is
much bigger than paychecks.

It's easy to get this whole "work hard" thing all twisted,
though. Our motives easily morph into wanting more instead
of wanting our Maker, taking things to an extreme that God
did not intend. It's easy to fall into the trap of believing that in
order to get ahead, we can't rest—except on an occasional vacation (where we take our cell phones and laptops to the pool so
we don't get behind)—and then when we are sixty-five, we can
retire and *slow down*.

Have you found yourself unable to slow down lately for fear that
everything will fall apart? Fill in the blank with how you feel below:

If I were to slow down now, even a little bit, I fear _____

_____.

In past years I lived in fear of never being good/popu-
lar/worthy/successful/accomplished enough. I thought that

working around the clock and never taking a break was something to be praised. Oh, friend, those days were so hard. And so unproductive in the big picture. I believed that the number in my bank account and the number of followers I had on social media somehow equated to my worth—and in order to increase those numbers, I had to increase my work hours and decrease rest. But where was that really getting me?

Think on these questions below for a moment, and be honest with yourself. Remember that honesty about where you are will help you leap to what's next:

- What is your current success equation?
- What numbers are you trying to increase?
- Why are you trying to increase them?
- How is all of this making you feel?

God designed good work coupled with good rest. He did not design the extremes of busy and lazy. And He gives us a way out of both.

Busy means having a great deal to do, which is not a bad thing in many cases. But when the things we are spending our time on aren't purposeful—when we use busy as an excuse, or when being busy begins to rule our lives—that's when things get messy. I'm defining *busy* in this context as the kind of busy that edges out intentional living. It's a kind of busy I know well.

Busy stems from the fear of never being enough. Busy strives, going to unhealthy extremes. If we stay busy, how can our lives be meaningless, right? We are full, packed, booked, needed, scheduled, and pulled from all directions. Busy covers our emptiness. Busy says, *I am in control.* Busy's sister, Lazy, is cut from the same cloth, but expresses herself in a different way. Lazy stems from that same fear of never being enough and apathetically withdraws. Lazy is often afraid to fail, try, or be anything significant. Lazy says, *Someone else can do the work.*

You may feel the same way I did, that being busy—working at the expense of everything else—is admirable, temporary, and necessary. But busy keeps us from making real life happen.

Stop the glorification of busyness. The More Work + More Work = Success equation does not add up, no matter how you stack your figures. You could even be doing a whole lot of good, purposeful work, but never resting can leave you exhausted, going through the motions to try to get through. Your work will suffer. Purpose will dwindle in favor of survival. Life is too short to spend an entire season working hard, thinking you'll live later. *Later* may never come, and you may find yourself working 24-7 forever at the expense of what matters most. You may feel your life completely slipping away, like I did.

Who says you have to work seven days a week to get ahead? Who made the rule that you have to scrape to the top to be successful? Who says you can't take a break?

Who made up these rules? Not God. If God—the Creator of heaven and earth—rested from all His work (Genesis 2:2), who are we to think that we don't need rest too?

The world says:

My Life + More Work = Financial Success and Lasting Happiness

God offers us a different equation for a true success and a purposeful life:

My Life + God's Way = Living On Purpose

God's way is the way of purpose. Of living intentionally in order to love others.

God's way is the way of rest coupled with meaningful work.

God's way is the way of true balance and lasting success.

God's way is not about us. God's way means less of us and more of Him.

God's way isn't always easy, but it's worth it.

Following God's success equation means you always have Him there to turn to and ask for guidance when you lose your way. God's way brings freedom, joy, and contentment.

What would your life look and feel like if you followed God's math instead of the world's?

Would your ability to love, give, and make what matters happen increase if you coupled good rest with intentional work? Would you be better for your family, friends, spouse, clients?

Is the thought of this totally overwhelming? Stay with me here, friend. I felt the same way at first.

Following God's true success equation eliminates busy and lazy and replaces them with intentional work and a deeper rest than you can get from a tropical island. How? Read on.

GETTING TIME BACK

It took redoing all my figures and examining my debts to get me to this realization, starting with my time boundaries—or rather, them. How you spend your time is how you spend your life, and I needed mine back.

If you need your time back, too, here are three guidelines as you take action:

1. Focus on progress, not perfection.
2. If you are overwhelmed, start small. Sometimes the hardest part is *starting*. Start somewhere.
3. Or start big. Dive in and make the big change you know you need to make.

Whether you start small or big, there's no one-size-fits-all plan. Do whatever it takes to make what matters happen, starting today!

Start small or start big, but make sure you *start*. Life is too short and too valuable to wait. For me, committing to not working *at all* on Sundays was completely overwhelming. I had to take this little by little. I started with one small (but huge for me at the time) step in the right direction toward living on purpose: one Sunday off.

My fear: I am afraid that if I slow down even for this one day, everything will fall apart, and I will have nothing left. No money, no business, no comfort, no marriage, no self-worth. I am afraid everything will crash, and I'll get behind, and people will think I'm a total failure.

The leap: I surrender one day of my life—a full Sunday away from work—in order to open my life and marriage to God. Something has to change!

If I don't leap: Our marriage might never be put back together, and I'll keep going on this destructive path.

If I leap and this fails: I'll probably cry, but I will try something else. This is worth it. I can't keep living this way.

Write out your action plan too:

My fear:

The leap:

Then weigh the risks versus the possible regrets you may have:

If I don't leap:

If I leap and this fails:

I hoped that giving up control over one day of my life would be my new beginning. I wish I could say it wasn't a big deal, but I knew it would be hard and that I'd be tempted by work, so I did everything I could to set myself up for success. I texted friends to let them know I was going offline for a day. I put my computer under my bed and opened the Bible on my desk in its place. I made a list of things I should do if Ari was busy and I got tempted by work: call Mom on the house phone, take a walk outside, and go through my closet to find clothes to donate. I even removed the battery from my cell phone and stuck it in my desk drawer with a note that read, "You can do this!" Turning it off wasn't enough; I had to remove its power source.

What can you do to set yourself up to live *on purpose?* Write three small, actionable ideas below. The more specific you are, the better. For example, instead of listing "Take a day off," write out the specific day you plan to take off (or even an hour off to start small) and what purposeful, intentional things you will do with your time. Be sure this plan is realistic. Do what you can, but make sure you do *something.* This will be worth it!

1.

2.

3.

MAKING PROGRESS

Being constantly busy had become so routine for me that Ari thought something was wrong when I came home from church and asked if he wanted to go get lunch. "Don't you have to work?" he asked. "I already have plans with friends." Realizing that our lives were still very separate, despite my individual decision to change, was hard. I wanted things to be better right away, but they weren't. I couldn't change Ari; all I could do was commit to changing myself, no matter how many times I messed up or what his reactions were.

A friend who knew about our strained marriage had given us a book called *The Love Dare,* a forty-day challenge to help

couples understand the practice of unconditional lo͞
time available allowed me to open the book instead of m͞ɣ ͞
that day. If I was going to risk taking all this time off work, I figured, I at least needed to *try* to make our marriage better.

The first "love dare" seemed simple enough: say nothing
negative to your spouse for one full day. I decided to give it a
whirl. I thought of myself as a positive person, but my words
quickly told me otherwise. I bit my tongue so much that I barely
had anything left to say. If our words are a mirror to our souls,
mine was in need of deeper repair than I had expected.

Dare number two: do one unexpected gesture of kindness
for your spouse, not expecting anything in return. *Okay, I can
do this one.* Every day for one week I did something small, like
a love note on a sticky note or a random hug even when I didn't
feel like it. This was hard. I still felt so much anger and resentment toward him for all the past hurts. Writing "I love you" on a
sticky note felt like getting my teeth cleaned. It was not as easy
as I had thought it would be.

Then again, nothing truly rewarding is ever easy.

I didn't tell Ari I was reading the book or what I was doing. I
just took action. After watching two hours of *SportsCenter* with
him one night and asking about football ("How many quarters
are there in a game?"), I could feel something changing in the air.
The next day Ari came home with flowers for me "just because."
There was no perfect marriage waiting for me when I put down
the cell phone and laptop, but even so, we were making major
progress.

Write this guideline down somewhere where you will see it often.
Maybe even make it your computer desktop or your iPhone back-

ground, or put it on a sticky note and tack it to the inside of your fridge so you remember what matters:

Progress, not perfection.

QUESTION EVERYTHING

This little bit of progress in our marriage led me to question the way I was doing *everything*.

Why was I doing things the way I was doing them?

How could I simplify?

How could I live more on purpose?

The goal: purpose, not perfection.

I was still working many late nights, e-mailing people at all hours, and then I would be frustrated when they e-mailed me back during those same hours. I e-mailed clients on weekends, which taught them they could e-mail me on weekends and expect a reply. I felt obligated to reply immediately, out of fear that I wasn't pleasing them. Does this sound familiar to you?

But then it dawned on me: How do people feel when they see an e-mail time-stamped with 3:00 a.m.? Even 9:00 p.m.? I put myself in their shoes. First, they think, *Oh, great! I can e-mail her anytime I want because she is probably awake and working.* In the same breath, they may think, *Wow! She has no structure, no time management skills, and no personal life.* While some may think, *Wow! She works hard;* the vast majority would say, *She's working too hard.*

If you have a business, do you want your customers to think of you as unbalanced? Is imbalance something you want to keep *living*? A life of purpose creates boundaries that give you more balance, which affects everything you do and everyone you work with. *Boundaries help you raise the bar.* I was so fearful, at first, to set a structure. I thought if I wasn't available 24-7, I'd lose business. Instead, the opposite happened. I started seeking the type of client I knew would respect my boundaries, and my quality of work improved.

I summoned my courage to take another leap: no social media or e-mail on weekends. This was huge for me. It wasn't about setting a rule; it was about setting a boundary around something that was distracting me from real life. And you know what happened? When I stopped sending e-mails on weekends, I received far less weekend e-mails—I wasn't supplying anything for people to respond to!

I took another huge leap, giving up the fear of not pleasing people for the possibility that I might get more valuable time back, and I set office hours. I put them in my e-mail signature and in my auto reply, and I communicated them to anyone who would listen. If, for some reason, I answer anything later than normal, it doesn't get sent out till the next morning. I turn my e-mail to "offline" after hours, and then at nine the next morning, I let those e-mails go out. I set the tone for when I am available via e-mail. I don't want to take calls after hours, so I don't call people after hours. I don't want to receive urgent e-mails on weekends, so I don't send them myself. *This changed my life.*

Do I ever break these boundaries? Yes. If a friend needs personal help at midnight, I'm there. It's not about rules; it's about following God's heart and making room for what matters.

When I started working less and trying to do the things God was telling me to do, I became a better boss. I gave people better business advice. I made clearer business decisions that were based on long-term growth. Sticking to healthy boundaries will make you *more* productive. If you know your workday ends at 6:00 p.m., you'll work hard every hour before that. Knowing I don't work on weekends now, I work my tail off during the week to get it all done. It's so worth it. Saying no to one thing is saying yes to another. There is a difference between busy and productive. The less busy and the more purposeful and focused I became, the more my life and business grew in the right direction.

That first full weekend I took off—no phone, no e-mails, no posts, no tweets, no likes—was the weekend Ari and I spent exploring local gardens together and laughing over takeout in the kitchen. One weekend turned into two weekends, which gave me such joy come Monday that I finally weeded through my inbox with a machete. For the first time in the two years we had been in North Carolina, I felt this thing I had forgotten about because it was so foreign: I felt rested. I felt *hope*.

TAKE TIME FOR TIME OFF

What about you? Does taking time off seem overwhelming? The less-work equation seems so counterintuitive at first and so impossible when you are deep in the thick of bills and mountains of e-mails. I get it. So start small.

Plan what matters. Use the days you've been given on purpose. Here are some ideas to get you started today:

1. START WITH ACTIVE REST DURING YOUR DAY

Set a timer for sixty minutes. Work for sixty minutes as hard as you can, then take a ten-minute break to do absolutely no work. If you can, step away from your computer completely, no matter how much work you have left. Take a walk, lie down, have a dance party in your office, or, if you're able, walk out of the building and get some fresh air.

Here's the deal, though: no checking e-mail (even personal), no social media, no Internet. Just take a break with your head out of your phone and computer. Take some deep breaths. Get some water, stretch, eat some healthy food, read a few pages of a good book. Let your mind focus on what matters most—whatever it is that connects you right back to God. Get creative! The only rule is to stay away from the Internet.

I didn't make this up. There is significant research that says doing bouts of focused work during the day and taking real breaks—active rest—makes your productivity and focus skyrocket. We do this in my office and it just plain works. I encourage the women I work with to take breaks—go get coffee, have lunch, take a walk—anything. A five-minute walk around the block is like a miracle for our focus. Even when I just walk out to get the mail and come back, I feel more refreshed and ready to work with more focused intention.

2. SCHEDULE A DAY OFF

Trust me; when you know you aren't working on Sunday, you work much harder and smarter during the week to get it all done. When I know I'm committed to not e-mailing on the weekends or after 6:00 p.m., I get it done during the day. I make it happen. No distractions allowed. The crazy thing is, my work-load has tripled in the last three years, and I'm getting triple the amount of work done—and done well—because I am planning active rest ahead of time.

Even if it's a month from now, look at your calendar, write

down a day you will take completely off from work, and make it happen. From someone who spent the first seven years in business working seven days a week, I know how hard this challenge is. It doesn't have to be every week at first, but I guarantee you will see the benefits in your life and in your work, and you will want to start taking more time off to refuel. It will become essential to your productivity. You will get more done in half the time. I want you to try it at least once. That's doable, right? Just one day off. Build from there.

3. PLAN A FULL WEEKEND OFF

Stay with me here! Even if you stay home, take a weekend completely away from technology: Internet, TV, phone. Plan several of these in the next twelve months. If you think it's impossible right now, make a plan for the future. Note these weekends on your calendar, and take action steps to make them happen. You *can* do this. Life is too short to miss it in e-mails and unfocused days. So start small and plan ahead.

These three action steps are simply a kick-start. My hope is that you will feel like I did, and like the thousands who have taken these first steps with me. I hope and pray that you will experience a tiny glimpse of the true success equation and never look back.

PRAYING THE IMPOSSIBLE

I was no longer working on weekends, and Ari and I were spending more time together. I prayed, *What else do I need to do, God? Can't you flip a switch and make our marriage perfect now?* He had certainly made us better, but *better* was relative.

Better meant we had some great days, where we didn't scream at each other. Those days were water to our parched hearts, but there had been a drought for so long that it was going to take more than a few weekends to heal our marriage. I started to pray the impossible: "God, help Ari believe in You too."

I knew I couldn't change Ari, but God could. I read about people in the Bible who prayed big prayers and believed in God's promises against all logic. God wants *everyone* to know Him, so why not my husband?

I couldn't make Ari believe in God by throwing Bible verses at him, but I could try to make him *feel* Him. God worked in me to show Ari His love, not by my might but by my surrender. When we fought, my default was to lash back at him for the hurtful things he said and not talk to him for hours. But I knew God was changing me—loving me into a new way to live—and He wanted me to show Ari His love in action.

When a fight swelled, I would swallow my pride, pray for wisdom, and tell Ari, "I love you." At first, he would be angry when I said that, claiming it was unfair. But after dozens more fights and about thirty "I love yous," he finally started to believe me.

It is often said that a great marriage takes work. This is true, but the work of marriage is the work of surrendering—taking giant leaps of faith and working hard every day to love on purpose. It's the kind of work that multiplies love and hope in others too. God calls us to love deeply and serve each other as He served us—giving our lives for the sake of another.

Gradually the layers of hurt and resentment and pain began to melt. Ari and I started fighting *for* our marriage. We began sleeping in the same bed again. It had been almost a year by that point. It was awkward at first and felt as though we were getting to know each other all over again, but this was a clear sign to me that God was indeed working on both of our hearts.

SURRENDERING TO GOD'S WORK

We committed to learning more about each other's lives in order to grow closer. Ari wanted me to understand his work, so I came to visit him at the hospital. I, in turn, summoned my courage and asked him to join me at church one Sunday. Hesitantly, he agreed.

I was so nervous, not wanting him to be turned off or offended in any way. I fretted as the service began. *I hope they play good songs. Will Ari like the sermon? Please no one mention Jesus too much!* Then I realized how completely ridiculous my thoughts were. I couldn't control what Ari was going to experience that morning. I let go.

I took a leap of faith, choosing to believe in something bigger than me. In that moment, and many more to follow, I battled my doubts and chose *possible* over *impossible.*

Now is your time to do the same.

Friend, the seemingly impossible things are a no-brainer for God. Whether your impossible is a fresh start, a new job, a healed relationship, a simplified schedule, or something even bigger, God has it. But we have to do our part and live in His success equation, opening margin in our days to be able to say *yes* when He says *go!* When we surrender our schedules and trade busy for bold faith, real life opens up.

Take action. Jesus didn't come and wave a magic wand to save us; He came to *do* something—something that showed us what real love and sacrifice are. He came to give it all—serving, giving, teaching, and showing us how to live on purpose. Whatever it is in your life that needs to be surrendered, changed, or set free, His success equation always wins.

My Life + God's Way = True Success.

Always.

Making it happen means ~~following~~ the REAL Success equation.

TAKE ACTION

▶ Go to LaraCasey.com/makeithappen to download an art print that reads: *How you spend your time is how you spend your life.* Print it out and place it somewhere prominent as a reminder to focus on the real success equation.

▶ Write out what your life might look like if you lived by the real success equation. What might be different? How would you feel? Write it down in detail.

▶ Do the three action steps you wrote in the "Take Time for Time Off" section of this chapter. As you carve out rest in your day, week, and year on your calendar, you will discover that these rest times will help you to connect to what matters most.

11

MAKE ROOM FOR GRACE

Nothing is impossible with God.
EVER.
PERIOD.
END of STORY.

I was committed to applying God's success equation to every part of my life, but I couldn't do it alone. I needed friends— good friends I could grow in faith with and talk to about God. To keep growing in my faith, I knew I needed people in my life who were committed to growing in theirs as well.

But how was I going to find people I could relate to as a business owner who also loved God? I was too timid to open myself up to people while my heart was still very fragile. The only thing I could think to do was pray. *God, I don't know where or how to find good friends, but I know I need them. Please help me find them.*

A wedding planner e-mailed me one afternoon, asking how I made so many things—so many businesses and a personal life—happen. I started to e-mail her back when I sensed it would be better if I blogged my response to her to try others as well. My post was the flat-out vulnerable truth about my new success equation and how I thought about life now. I was nervous about posting it because it was the first time I had talked about my faith online, and I certainly wasn't perfect. The question from my training days kept interrupting me: *How can I lead when I'm still learning?* I prayed and prayed. Shaking, I hit Publish on a blog post titled "How to Make Things Happen, Vol. 1."

Hundreds of comments, e-mails, calls, and texts began pouring in. God was showing me that it was possible to be broken *and* to help others. In fact, there was power in my vulnerability—it resonated with people. To this day, almost seven years later, I still get comments on that post.

People wanted to learn more, and I started to get overwhelmed again, answering hundreds of e-mails and spending hours on the phone doing individual consulting sessions. A friend called me one day to suggest that I start a workshop to teach these principles to groups. Thirty days later I took another leap of faith and announced a thirteen-city workshop tour. This would mean I'd be away from home for two weeks, but I'd help more people and get so much of my time back when I was home. It was a good exchange. The first Making Things Happen Tour sold out in two days.

During the very first Making Things Happen workshop, I met Emily Ley and Gina Zeidler, two women who wanted to live on purpose too. Emily was working a full-time job in nonprofit management at the time and really wanted to be a stationery designer. Gina worked in marketing, but she wanted to go full-time with photography. After that first workshop we talked on the phone often as both of them took leaps of faith to pursue the dreams God had for them. They inspired me, and I knew they would inspire others as well. I opened my heart to them, hoping they might be the answer to my prayers, and asked them to join me in leading the workshop for a second tour later that year.

Emily and Gina met me in Houston for our first stop. Hungry from our travels, we went straight to the hotel restaurant to eat. We sat down at the counter and ordered soup. Suddenly, Gina's tears poured out with her words: "Lara, since we're going to spend a lot of time together these next weeks, I need to tell you something." I was taken aback by her emotion and had no idea what was coming next. "When we met for the first time for coffee, you were forty-five minutes late. I felt like I wasn't important to you at all. You didn't even apologize when you finally showed up."

My heart sank. I felt resentful and wanted to reply, "I opened my heart and took a big risk to have you come on this tour with me to build a friendship with you, and you start things off by railing into me?" But then I remembered all God was doing in my life, and my fervent prayers for genuine relationships. This was my chance to turn things around and take a risk toward vulnerability. I took a deep breath and put myself in her shoes, realizing I had unknowingly and carelessly hurt her. "Gina, I am so sorry," I started. "I didn't mean to hurt you, and I'm so sorry."

We kept talking through the hurt. I sat back and listened with my heart instead of my defensive ego. In that painful exchange, the seed of a true friendship was sown. Over the long hours spent in airports and hotels through Phoenix, Chicago, Atlanta, Los Angeles, and Maui (and dozens of cities in years ahead), God answered my prayer. Gina and Emily are friends who tell me when I am wrong and pray fervently for me. Our friendship has been through so many trials, and those challenges have always made us stronger because we know our shared purpose.

FROG KICKS

During one of the Making Things Happen tours, Gina, Emily, and I visited my Grandma Bunny in Irvine, California. Emily was seven months pregnant, and the little one in her belly was kicking up a storm throughout our travels. At Grandma's house I sheepishly asked Emily if I could put my hand on her belly to feel the baby kicking.

Ari and I had just started sleeping in the same bed again, so babies seemed a long way off. We casually talked about having kids someday, when he was done with his residency and fellowship in about five years. I placed my hands on Emily's belly and felt baby Brady's frog kicks. At that moment God planted a seed in my heart that it was time—despite all my logic—to think about having a baby.

Ari and I were nervous, but something in us knew it was time.

Three weeks later, there were two pink lines.

God was clearly at work. It was a miracle but a terrifying one at times. I felt a heightened urgency. *How are we going to have a baby when our marriage is just starting to get better? How am I going to keep working and be a mom too?* I feared not being prepared. I feared this rhythm I had found with my work and life would completely fall apart. Business was great, and my staff was happy, yet I feared what would happen without me there to run things.

As the morning sickness intensified, this life-altering truth pressed into my heart with every beat: God had formed a new life from both of ours. From two broken people who were slowly being put back together. If God can take broken pieces and make something new out of them, why shouldn't I trust Him with *all my life*? Why would I worry or fear what was next? He wanted me to let go of my own life for a better one ahead.

Do you fear what's next? Are you worried about the unknown? That's okay. God knew we would face these challenges often, so He gave us lots of reminders in His Word to help us find trust and peace about the future. One of my favorite passages is Matthew 6:25–27:

> Therefore I tell you, do not worry about your life, what you will eat or drink; or about your body, what you will wear. Is not life more than food, and the body more than clothes? Look at the birds of the air; they do not sow or reap or store away in barns, and yet your heavenly Father feeds them. Are you not much more valuable than they? Can any one of you by worrying add a single hour to your life?

That last line always gets me. What can be gained by worrying?

I often worry when I don't know what the outcome of a challenging situation will be, and I want to gain control. But what if today's worries are opportunities for deeper faith?

In your times of worry, seek Him—pray, read His word, sing to Him, paint for Him, whatever it is that draws you close—and watch Him turn your worry into trust and peace.

MAKING TIME FOR WHAT MATTERS

The more round my belly grew, the more my worries about letting go threatened to crush me. It was time to surrender to even more change. Big change. Sometimes you have to say no to one thing in order to say yes to something better.

I took a financial risk and closed my event planning business. It was hard, but I knew I had to close one door so another could open. I put a stop on travel and speaking engagements, clearing my calendar for the months ahead. We stopped touring the Making Things Happen workshop and now do it in a conference format twice a year here in my home city of Chapel Hill. I turned down two dream speaking engagements in Ireland and nineteen others. I closed the consulting company I had at the time. These were all big financial risks when we really needed to be making more income to save for having a baby, but the risk was worth it. I decided I would rather eat beans every day than not have time for what matters.

Ari and I read Dave Ramsey's *The Total Money Makeover*, made a household budget, and started hunting for a used car to replace my fancy sports car lease. I became aware of how wasteful I had been. We had two huge yard sales. I began cooking at home every night. I wanted to welcome our daughter to arms of parents who lived intentionally. I knew I wouldn't be perfect, but perfect wasn't the goal. Letting go of my life for a better one—my ways for God's ways—was my aim.

God showed me in all this that He will always provide what I really need. What I needed more than my stuff or money was *time*.

I started saying no in order to open my time and space to something better. The more of my life I surrendered, the more life started to happen—for both of us. Ari began to wonder where all this change was coming from. He came to church with me more often. This opened us to many conversations about faith and our marriage. Through it all, I could feel God reminding me, *Lara, the impossible is possible. Believe in what you can't yet see.*

What about you? What "impossible" thing are you praying for God to do right now?

Are you open to waiting for God to make things happen in His way and in His time?

It's on the way from where we are to where we're going that we learn to trust God. It's in the middle of what feels hopeless that, in our complete surrender, life happens.

IS THIS REALLY HAPPENING?

My trust in God and fear of not being in control came in waves. My due date was growing closer. The need for control began to swell. I got the house in order and read every book I could find on parenting and childbirth, trying to ensure that nothing would go wrong when the baby came. I had the *perfect* birth plan typed out. Even my due date was perfect: 11.11.11. My parents had flown in the day before to be there. It was going to be magical. *God, no big challenges after the baby comes, please! I have everything under control.*

The due date came, and nothing happened. The next day, nothing. I was so frustrated. I was anxious and tired and *very* pregnant.

Ari was already on his scheduled paternity leave, and we were burning it up by the day. Eight days past my due date, Ari said to me, "Do you think the baby's coming today? Phil asked me to have lunch with him." Phil was a preacher from our church. Even if the baby was coming that day, I didn't care. Just months before, Ari was uncomfortable having a Bible in our house, and now he was having lunch with Phil, the *preacher*?

I knew God was up to something, so I tried to play it cool: "Sure, go ahead."

I decided to pray instead of waste any more time in worry. Letting go of control, I prayed a big prayer: "Please help Ari to believe in You before I have this baby."

That night, around 3:00 a.m., in my restless sleep I noticed a light on the other side of the bed. Ari was reading something on his phone. Odd. I tried to fall back asleep. Two hours later the glow was still there. *What on earth is he reading all night long?*

The next night, nine days after my due date, I woke to the same thing. Ari's face glowed as he read something on his phone screen that captivated him. My curiosity was killing me. I scooted over toward him to peek at the screen.

I thought for a moment that perhaps this was a dream. *Could it be? God, is this really happening?* Ari was reading the Bible.

The next morning I woke to the unmistakable rhythm of contractions. It was time.

HER NAME

We named her Grace—a fitting reminder of what God had given us: the gift of a strengthened marriage and, for me, a new desire to live on purpose.

She was perfect, but I remember feeling fragile and sad the first days in the hospital after she was born. I kept thinking, *This is supposed to be the happiest occasion ever! Why do I feel so off?*

When my parents had to fly back to Florida and Ari had to go back to work, I sat in the living room with Grace in my arms and wept. *How am I going to do this by myself? I have no idea what I'm doing. What if I mess up? I'm not cut out for this!*

When Grace cried, I felt helpless. I couldn't control things or fix her. I stayed up for most of the night, protectively watching her and making sure she was breathing. I felt as though I wasn't meant to be a mom.

Sleep-deprived arguments with Ari flared. I cried and whined to God, wondering why I had to go through so much anguish. *Why can't things just be easy? Why am I going through this?*

No one told me that babies don't express love until they're about three months old. This was so hard for me. It was like loving a brick wall—a brick wall that cried a lot.

God was breaking me down to build me back up stronger, new and reliant on Him, not on my circumstances. He was preparing me for something much bigger than me.

In the early months of motherhood, as I loved on a baby who couldn't yet love me back, I realized a powerful truth: that's exactly how God feels about *you and me.* He loves and gives and nurtures and soothes, and sometimes we don't even acknowledge Him. He loves us unconditionally anyway. He gives and gives and gives, no matter what we do.

Take a moment to thank God for His unconditional and constant love, comfort, and care for you.

At my five-week postpartum checkup, I told my how I had been feeling. He encouraged me to get more sleep. Meaning, I *had* to let go of feeling like I had to be awake, making sure Grace was okay every five minutes. I had to put my trust in God 100 percent.

There were beautiful moments in those first weeks too. I relished those times because they temporarily erased all the rest. I loved the way Grace's little head smelled like heaven. Her skin was so soft.

Grace was wonderful. I had nothing to complain about and *everything* to be grateful for when it came to her. My postpartum depression had nothing to do with the baby; it had everything to do with my expectations and desire to control my life. My heart needed to change to be able to let her in.

I kept questioning God, wondering why I was so very far from my former self. I felt like I'd never ever get my life back—and the thing was, I wouldn't. God had a better self in mind.

ARI'S FAITH

Struggling to find strength to help with the baby and still be his best at work on no sleep, Ari sought advice from his new friend Phil, the preacher from lunch. Phil and his wife, Leslie, had gently weaved themselves into our lives, knowing we needed help. They selflessly served us. They knew Ari was not a Christian, but they never made him feel like an outsider. Phil had the same dry sense of humor as Ari. They became great friends—best friends, in fact.

It was in the safety of his relationship with Phil, and through seeing God's love in action, that Ari's heart was changed. I never thought I would type these next words: Ari became a believer exactly two months after Grace's birth. The impossible happened.

Your impossible can happen, too, friend. God is big and real and good. His desire is that we would all come to know His transforming grace.

We began the process of healing and forgiving each other for the hurts of our past through the lens of our new shared faith. It took time and counsel and much prayer, but God is faithful. His grace has and continues to flip every iota of our lives upside-down as we get to know His heart more and more. We aren't perfect, but we now know our purpose.

Because of what I've experienced in my own marriage and life, the work I do—the heartbeat of our company—is now driven on this truth: the impossible is possible. No matter how lost or forsaken you feel, God's love never fails. He can change what feels unchangeable. God is real and always at work, even if everything in your life is telling you otherwise right now. Don't just pray about what seems logical and possible. Pray hard about the impossible.

Making it happen means being OPEN to God's timing + GRACE.

TAKE ACTION

▶ Write out the "impossible" prayers that came to mind earlier in the chapter. Be honest. Be bold. Take a big leap and lay them out on paper. These prayers may feel too impossible to write or say, so we never utter them. Give them life right now by writing them down.

▶ Go to LaraCasey.com/makeithappen to download an Amazing Grace art print for your home or office. May this be a reminder to you that His grace can change everything!

12

FOLLOW HIM

Follow
~~YOUR DREAMS~~
Him

I used to live my life by the kinds of inspirational quotes I often saw circulating online:

- Follow your dreams.
- Do more of what makes you happy.
- Follow your dreams, and they will come true.
- Follow your dreams; they know the way.
- There is no set path. Just follow your heart.

But as I have shared with you in this book, following my heart led me to believe I was not enough, I would never be free of fear, and I was *worthless*. Following my heart led me to almost lose my marriage. It pains me to think of the potential consequences of that happening—I wouldn't have Ari, Grace, or the heartbeat that drives *Southern Weddings*.

Nowhere in the Bible did God say, "Follow your dreams" or "Follow your heart." He simply said, "Follow Me."

If you are hesitant to surrender to those two life-giving words, the next three sentences are perhaps the most important I will write to you in these pages: Following Him frees us from chasing perfect. Following Him frees us from a life going nowhere. Following Him gives us a clear life-giving *purpose*—to love Him and serve others so they know that love too.

There was a time in my dark younger days when I was at a club in Las Vegas, surrounded by thousands of people dancing to the deafening beat. Everything went silent for a split second, and I felt God asking, *What are you doing here, Lara?*

Years later He keeps asking that question of me, and He's asking you too.

What are you doing here?

What are you doing with your days, hours, minutes here on this earth?

What are you doing with the gifts He has given you?

How are you using your life: by accident or on purpose?

ARE YOU PURSUING HAPPINESS OR HIM?

When I was following my own dreams and desires instead of God's, my motivating force and reason for being was to be happy. I thought that's what we were supposed to do: life, liberty, and the pursuit of *happiness*, right? So I would wake each morning thinking, *What can I do/eat/buy that will make me feel happy* d I found a lot of pleasure—it's not hard to come by in __. But as soon as those happy-inducing things were gone or circumstances changed, I'd be back to running on empty.

When we feel empty, we can fill the void with what lasts or with what doesn't last. God's plan is for us to fill the void with Him. He wants us to know Him. In fact, He designed us to know Him. And when we choose Him over the world, little by little—and sometimes in great waves—life gets better; relationships are formed, love prevails, and we find the lasting joy of community.

God's version of true happiness is so much better than what our culture presses toward. While everyone around you might be happily overspending, overindulging, or rising to the top of the success ladder at any cost, there is a much greater reward for those who follow a different path. The goal is not happiness; the goal is *Him.*

Fleeting pleasures last only for a moment. When something challenging would happen in my life, I used to think, *Well, at least I have money. At least my business is still doing well. At least I still have all this stuff. At least I still have all these followers on Twitter.* Then God shook those things up to get me to see the truth. The source of true contentment, something that challenges my faith daily, is simply this: I have God. I have all I need. He never changes. His love and mercy are always there. Your house and your stuff and your money and your status and your youth won't last forever, but His love never fails—it never dies or fades. Putting our hope in the eternal is far more fulfilling than fleeting happiness.

Are you pursuing happiness or Him? Write out all the areas of your life where you invest your time and energy. Examples: vocation, family, health, finances, friendships, etc. Then, be even more specific in each category. For example, under *vocation* you might list *marketing, blogging, office supplies, social media, business finances,* etc. Finally, next to each area, write whether you are seeking happiness or Him. Pray that God will give you wisdom to know how to surrender *every* aspect of your life to Him.

Pursuing happiness instead of God led me to live a very isolated life. I compared my worth against others' and strove to be better than them. Now I know that following Him brings us into community—it gives us dear friends and true family.

God's purpose flips life and achievement on their heads. He makes the mundane meaningful and gives us deep contentment in challenges. His purpose gives us a focus. Following God doesn't make us perfect; it makes us *purposeful,* filling our emptiness and equipping us to take focused action on what matters. His purpose helps us know what's truly important and where *not* to put our attention.

What about you? Fill in the blanks:

Chasing happy/perfect makes me feel _____.

Living on purpose makes me feel _____.

I thought that when I finally found happiness, my life would be simpler. When I finally had the perfect house, car, job, and amount of money, that's when I could finally breathe. Pursuing happiness kept me busy but left me feeling overwhelmed and worn out. But as I gradually learned, following Him is better than *doing it all* because we start *doing what matters*.

USE YOUR GIFTS ON PURPOSE

God's purpose for us is painted in every letter of the Bible, and it can be summed up in this: *love God and serve people*. He has given us all different gifts, talents, and resources to use for carrying out this purpose. God's purpose for us is the big-picture vision; goals are our action plans to carry out that vision, using all He has given us.

God's big vision made me want to set goals so that I could live my life *on purpose*, using all the gifts and resources He has given me to love Him and serve others. I have to keep reminding myself to set goals that fuel *His* purpose, not my own gain or what someone else says is a worthy pursuit. I mess up all the time, but the pursuit of living on purpose is *worth it*.

Have you felt the pressure to realize someone else's dreams for you or to live up to someone else's expectations for your life?

Take a moment to write your experience out.

Publishing a magazine is something I do, but it's not my purpose. If I lost my job, I wouldn't lose my purpose. Purpose doesn't go to work; it goes to love. God wants us to live on purpose—wholeheartedly with focused intention—no matter where we are. Living on purpose doesn't mean having your dream job; it means being all there right where you are. Take every opportunity to be a light for Him. This is not to say that you can't or shouldn't take the leap to pursue another job, but many times there is opportunity to live on purpose right in front of us. God wants to do extraordinary things through our surrendered hearts and hands.

A note for mamas: you are never "just a mom." I hear this phrase echoed so often with an undertone of shame. There is no room for comparing the importance of our gifts with others' when our big-picture purpose is the same. We are all working to build God's kingdom, so all the parts and players are equally important.

Seeing life through the lens of purpose has changed the way I work, my relationship with money, my ability to care for people, the way I lead my staff, the way I parent, what I read—I could go on. Living on purpose is a *heart* change, not a lifestyle change. The change in lifestyle is a product of a truly converted heart. And I know I've only just begun this journey—God is never done with us.

THE "SECRET" TO LIFE

If there is a "secret" to life it's this: following God is far more valuable than all the riches and comforts in the world. Whatever you are going through right now, if it's humbling you, making you pray, bringing you to your knees, and making you feel like you cannot do this alone, maybe there is a reason—a glorious, beautiful reason.

Following Him means taking giant leaps of faith, giving up your ways for *the* way, your life for *the* life, your truth for *the* truth. Following Him may mean leaving your job, or it may mean staying right where you are. It may mean hard work, choosing to go to uncharted territory, and diving headfirst into your fears, but He never fails, and He has a very good plan.

"FOLLOW ME" IS A CALL TO ACTION

Jesus' call to us is very simple: *Follow Me.* It is a clear call to action.

Are you willing to give up the chase for perfect in favor of the one and only thing that will bring you true contentment? If you feel hesitant, focus on the alternative in what chasing perfect makes you feel. The fruit of following Him, on the other hand, is "love, joy, peace, patience, kindness, goodness, faithfulness, gentleness, self-control" (Gal. 5:22–23 ESV). Following Him takes worry and fear and replaces them with contentment and faith.

BEGIN TODAY

I don't need motivation to do my job. I am passionate about helping people know that anything is possible with God. I believe God wants all of us to know Him and be free of shame. I believe He has given us gifts that are meant to be used.

Where did I begin, and where can you? Find out what God's dreams are, and start dreaming and doing *with* Him. Read His Word. Spend time with Him. Talk to Him and listen. Spend time with other people who love Him. There are no other secret answers, and—as I told you from the start—perfection is not a prerequisite. Quite the opposite. If you are broken, lost, hurt, or flawed—and *all* of us are—God wants you to know His heart, and He will help you. When you begin to see His true heart, you are going to want more, my friend. You are going to want to *do* something about it.

In the next section you will begin to take action on your purpose. "Your Guide to Make It Happen" is a doable, action-oriented guide to help you apply the lessons you have learned so far in this book. These five practical steps will equip you to clear the clutter, set good goals, and take leaps of faith to make it happen.

God is working in you something *bigger than you*, and He will carry, help, comfort, encourage, lead, lift, soothe, prod, refine, break, and build you back up to help you walk on His narrow path . . . if you follow Him.

Countless people out there need you to make it happen. They need your talents, your heart, and your fullest potential to influence them for the Lord. You can't bring everyone to Jesus, but you can bring Jesus to everyone. First, though, bring yourself to the foot of His cross and lay it all at His feet. Ask Him what He wants you to do. Above all else—He is all we need.

I NEED

~~to make more money~~

~~to have more business~~

~~to get more followers~~

~~to be happier~~

~~to get things done~~

~~to be the best~~

~~to be perfect~~

Jesus.

TAKE ACTION

▶ Read the previous quote. Have you convinced yourself that you need to make more money, to have more business, to get more followers, to be happier, to get things done, to be the best, or to be perfect? Fill in the blank below with the things that are not as important as your relationship with Him, and then sign and date your declaration to make it personal:

All I need is Jesus, not _____.

▶ Before you move to the next section, where we will make purpose happen together, let go of any expectations of what you *should* write, say, or do, and let God plant His dreams in your heart. Many times those dreams are so big they can overwhelm us. But the people who followed God in the Bible did some radical things to live on purpose—and the things I've seen the most fruit from in my life all started as "I have this crazy idea" moments. God wants us to use the talents, skills, and gifts we have been given to bless others. And He wants us to do it *together*. Go to www.LaraCasey.com/makeithappen and join us as we walk through dreaming God's dreams together!

Making it happen means knowing all you really NEED is JESUS.

PART FOUR

Your Guide to MAKE IT HAPPEN!

HOW TO USE THIS GUIDE

Let's Do This!

I was once really good at killing plants. I'd see an orchid in the grocery store, buy it on a whim for my desk, and then four days later it would be bloomless. But I now have a thirty-foot vegetable bed on the side of our house and a genuine love for cultivating new life.

Over the years I have developed a love for gardening. God showed me how addicted to instant gratification I had been. I didn't want to tend to anything in my life, much less a plant grown from seeds. I wanted to have stuff that was already pretty. I didn't care if a plant died—I'd just buy another one. I didn't care if I lost friends; I'd just get new ones. I didn't care if I had no life behind the scenes as long as everything looked perfect on the surface. I didn't care if my marriage suffered, if my business was succeeding. I didn't want to do hard work or get my hands dirty—I just did whatever was easy and instant.

When we surrender our fears, take leaps of faith, and begin living on purpose, God fills us, and we begin to cultivate what matters. He changes us for good. He makes us respect and relish the process of growth. Enjoying a tomato I grew in my own garden is like sharing a feast with God. I think of the months of watering, the hot summer days I spent pruning, and the bounty of sun God provided as I savor each bite. My gratitude now overflows. He made me want to get my hands dirty, commit to cultivating, and step into the hard stuff of life—broken relationships, failures, challenges—in order to give them *all* to Him. He made me love the process of planting, tending, and harvesting in my marriage, friendships, parenting, finances, business—everything.

My life before knowing God was set on instant gratification, and now, by His grace, I'm an imperfect, dirt-loving, fertilizer-spreading gardener.

When it comes to the process of creating a life of purpose, resist the urge to put yourself in an "I don't have a green thumb" box and give up before even trying. You don't have to actually garden as you go through this guide, but you may be surprised by what you will learn. The practice of gardening—whether a veggie bed, a cactus, or a Chia Pet—has the potential to teach you so much about God's heart and how He desires us to live.

CULTIVATE PURPOSE

You know what's amazing about plants? They give us food and make the world beautiful. And you know what's amazing about God? He makes our lives into gardens that are meant to be shared—inspiring others, nourishing them, and equipping them to live on purpose too.

Here are five steps to create a life of purpose:

1. Evaluate your life.
2. Clear the clutter.
3. Set purposeful goals.
4. Take action.
5. Encourage others.

You will go through each of these steps in this final section. Take your time as you work through the exercises. Getting through each one might take you a week or two—that's okay! In fact, the more time you take to make intentional decisions, the better. But let me also give you a swift kick in the pants: taking your time to be intentional doesn't mean procrastinating. Focus on progress, not paralyzing perfection. This process will be well worth it.

ESSENTIAL GARDENING RULES

As you begin this personal guide to making it happen, here are some helpful and essential gardening rules.

YOU CANNOT GROW ANYTHING WITHOUT LIGHT

I used to hate reading instructions. Even now, it can feel tedious when I want to get something done quickly. When I was a kid, my mom said I would put things together on my own with no instructions or help; I just wanted to do it *my* way. That was efficient in some cases, but later in my life it got me in a whole lot of trouble.

In gardening, we can't wing it—stuff will die, and we won't get the harvest we could potentially have. Likewise, we can't grow anything without God's light. We need His light in order to grow and to know where to go. There's no better how-to book for business, finance, parenting, marriage, and making life happen than the Bible. Read the instructions, do what they say, and watch what grows.

YOU CAN'T GROW THINGS IN A BUBBLE

Boundaries are important, but they cannot be impermeable walls. If you have put barbed wire around your life, keeping everyone and everything out, your garden will soon be sapped of life. Our gardens need protection from harmful intruders, but we also need bees to pollinate our plants. We need birds to help spread seeds. We need worms to till the soil. We miss out on so much goodness when we don't allow anyone or anything in. When the boundaries of our gardens allow for people to enter, people in need can be nourished. The bees, birds, and worms can get in and help you cultivate what matters. Have clear boundaries, but make sure they are purposeful, allowing for relationships and good growth.

YOU NEED A COMMUNITY OF PEOPLE FROM WHOM YOU CAN LEARN

We need other people who can teach us from their own experiences, encourage us when we get frustrated, and help us fix problems. Seasoned gardeners can help us understand the instructions so our gardens can flourish. I frequently ask my mom to decode plant-care instructions for me in terms I can understand. She knows from her own experience how to teach me effectively. Having a community of believers to grow with is essential.

GROW WHAT'S IN SEASON

Ultimately, God determines what flourishes and what dies in our lives. He may give you seasons of perfect growing weather, and He may send freak ice storms your way. Either way, you can trust that He has a plan, and it's bigger than we can understand. Your springs, summers, falls, and winters each present opportunities to plant, tend, harvest, or make room for what matters. Whatever season you're in, lean in.

KNOW THAT GOOD THINGS COME WITH TIME

New homeowners like trees labeled *fast growing* because they promise to fill a space in the yard quickly or help shade a sunny side of the house to decrease the cooling bill. But the wood of most fast-growing trees isn't as hard as their slow-growing sisters, and while what's above the surface may look tall and sturdy, their roots may not be established enough to withstand strong winds. Sometimes the most lasting things in our lives are those that grow slowly, over time, with great care and patience.

IN ORDER FOR SOMETHING NEW TO GROW, SOMETHING HAS TO DIE

In order for a seed to sprout, it must sacrifice itself, or die, in order to become a plant. The little seed casing must fall away for the tender, green, new life to appear. It is the same with our lives. Leaps of faith mean giving something up for the sake of something better, letting something die in order for something new to be able to grow. In the words of Jesus, who died for us on the cross, "Unless a kernel of wheat falls to the ground and dies, it remains only a single seed. But if it dies, it produces many seeds. Anyone who loves their life will lose it, while anyone who hates their life in this world will keep it for eternal life" (John 12:24–25). Let go of your life—and ways—for a much better one.

STEP 1: EVALUATE
YOUR LIFE

The first step to create a life of purpose is to evaluate how the garden of your life is doing, starting with where you are today. So grab a notebook and something to write with. Doing this section with a trusted friend or small group is really helpful too.

HOW ARE YOU?

Let's practice answering this important question from chapter 1: *How are you?* Allow yourself to be vulnerable and write or say the things that feel sticky. Vulnerability is where change begins. In order to leap into the new, we first must know where we are leaping from.

Your worries today can directly affect what you write next, so don't shove them under the table. Acknowledge them. Reply aloud, to a friend, or on paper right now. Choose whatever works best for you, but whatever you do, do it now. Don't wait.

Here are some prompts to help you:

- How are you feeling physically? (health, tension in your body, energy)
- How are you feeling about your work? (school, parenthood, a vocation)
- How are your relationships? (friendships, marriage, family)
- How are your finances? (relationship with money, financial health)
- How are you feeling about your creative passions, gifts, or talents? Are you using them?
- How are you feeling about your physical space?
- How are you feeling about your relationship with God?

One of the greatest gifts we can give one another is to listen, without trying to fix or control. If you are working through this guide with a friend or small group, give the gift of a listening ear. Allow others to say what's on their hearts, and let God do the responding. Pray for each other and love each other, but remember this is a process. Be still with your feelings—whatever they may be—without trying to change them or push them away immediately.

WHAT HAS BEEN WORKING?

Now let's take a look back at the last year. What grew well and produced fruit in your life? What are you grateful for from the last twelve months? What good things happened? I know this can be a challenging step for many. We don't like counting our blessings because it may feel self-indulgent or like it won't get us anywhere fast. But trust me here—it will.

It's easy to look back at an entire year and see only the yucky parts, like when something happens to you at the end of the day and you automatically call it a *bad* day, regardless of what happened the other twenty-three hours. Gratitude changes everything. Making your list of what went well can give you the energy and hope you need to press on full force. For me, it helps remind me that God is clearly at work, and I need to keep taking big risks for Him. Make this an exercise in praise.

A few tips on how to make your list of what has been working for you:

1. Talk to your significant other or a close friend about your year and ask him or her to reflect some of the highlights back to you. He or she may remember some that you have forgotten! This is also a wonderful way to celebrate the good things of the past year with others. Make it your dinner conversation tonight. And remember, this isn't all about you—ask others to tell you their highlights too. Build stronger connections by sharing what God is doing in your life.

2. Take a look back at your calendar, blog posts (if you blog), social media updates, or photos. Those might give you a clue into some of the highlights you've forgotten.

3. As you reflect on the good things this past year, say thank you not only to God but to those people who were a part of them. Whether through texts, e-mails, phone calls,

or physical letters, make gratitude happen! If you want a special gratitude letter to send to the people you love, print one out at www.LaraCasey.com/makeithappen.

Once you have your list of what worked, name three lessons you learned from what worked. For example, in my life there were many times last year that great things happened, when I let go of control—whether taking a different route than expected with a project, letting someone else lead, or letting myself make a mess. The lesson for me was a big one: let go and let God!

WHAT HASN'T BEEN WORKING?

What didn't work well for you this past year? What hindered you from living on purpose? What areas of your life need to be tended, watered, or soaked in sunshine? Don't just write or say, "Everything." Get specific and list your greatest challenges—the places that feel overgrown with impossible weeds right now. I know you want to make this your most purposeful year yet, so don't let negative self-talk paralyze you as you make this list. Write the facts and move forward. Each thing you write down is a potential area of your life you could surrender to God to make completely new.

Once you have your list, name three lessons you learned from what didn't work. For example, if you found yourself lost in worry a lot, perhaps the lesson is to trust in God more and have a list of key scriptures handy—on your desk, on your bathroom mirror, or by your bed—for times you feel worry coming on. Worrying is like praying for what you don't want.

WHAT ARE YOU AFRAID OF?

Like we talked about and practiced in chapter 2, meet your fear and name it in order to move past it. Imagine the worst-case-scenario outcome in your mind—that thing that you don't want to voice—and write it out:

I am afraid of _____ because

_____.

Rather than copy what you wrote before in chapter 2, write what's on your heart right now. Understanding our fears takes peeling back the layers, and that might take a lot of peeling. Keep going. There is good stuff waiting in every single layer you pull back. Surrender your real, honest fear to God. Write or say your honest fear, and know that you are not alone. Refer back to chapter 2 for the list of fears expressed by thousands of other women.

WHAT SEASON ARE YOU IN?

While writing this book, I found out we were pregnant with our second child. I was elated. The timing was perfect, and I was grateful Grace would have a sibling. Just weeks later I found myself in the emergency room, where a nurse practitioner examined me and tenderly said, "I'm so sorry, Lara. But know that you are not alone, and you will have another baby." I wept and pleaded with God, *Why? How did this happen?*

It had been an unusually hard winter already. We experienced several snowstorms, out of the norm for the sunny South.

My garden lay flat, filled with dried plant remnants instead of the blooms I remembered from summer. I spent cold days writing, battling what felt like oceans of fear and "not enough." *God, I don't want to share this or even write about it. I don't want to remember. And I am not a good writer. This book is going to fail. No one will be changed by this.*

I sensed God's response: *Write what I want you to write. Day by day, word by word, trust Me. Write My story in your life. I have a plan. All of this pain and failure led you to Me. Your past does not define you anymore; I do. Walk into the dead places of your life, and give them to Me. I will make them new.*

As we arrived home from the hospital—the same hospital where I would have given birth—I noticed little pieces of mulch popping up all over our yard. And then I saw them. From the dozens of bulbs I had planted in the fall, little green shoots were pushing up through the nothingness. Even when you can't see it, there is life beneath the desolate surface. After winter, no matter how hard or cold, always comes spring.

- In spring, new life appears out of what felt bleak. It's a time of planting, blooming, and celebration.
- In summer, we cultivate, prune, and tend. We get our hands dirty in the soil and work hard in the scorching heat.
- In fall, our crops bear fruit and bounty to share. We reap the harvest, uprooting our fields and clearing out life before the stillness of winter arrives.
- In winter, the frozen fields are bare, and the soil is still. Winter is a time we are drawn inside. It's a time of forced stillness, allowing us to reflect on our lives and how we can live them more fully in the seasons ahead.

What season are you in right now? Circle the season that best matches your life at the moment.

BE STILL

Stillness is hard, isn't it? We don't *want* to be still. We don't know if we can handle what's waiting in the stillness. It might be painful or overwhelming. We don't want to *feel*, period. We fear stillness won't be productive. We don't want to think or feel; we want to *do*.

But stillness is not the opposite of forward motion. In stillness we are able to hear powerful wisdom that gives us clarity. And clarity produces action. That's what we want, right? To know what to do. It may seem counterintuitive, but it's true: stillness enables us to move forward with purpose. Stillness allows us to be intentional instead of reactionary. Surrendering to stillness might be the most active, life-giving step you take.

Trust and be patient in the dry times or periods of slow growth. God is always at work. In every season He is at work. He is with you.

STEP 2: CLEAR THE CLUTTER

Every garden I've ever tended has had weeds. It's not that I've planted them—they simply come compliments of the dirt. Appearing in different shapes and sizes, they will choke out what's supposed to be growing if left unattended. So it's important to address them.

In the same way, to make things happen we must deal with the resident issues. Step 2 of our process calls for us to dig in a little deeper and identify what may be causing some of the challenging feelings or fears you've encountered.

IDENTIFY AND REMOVE THE WEEDS

Weeds are the things that try to suck the life out of us. They try to take over, choking new growth. Weeds distract us from our purposes, dividing our attention from what matters.

Weeds are tricky, though. You can't simply yank some of

them out of the ground, or you might pull up the good stuff with them. Many times I've pulled up huge chunks of good soil or even other plants—those little buggers have some crazy-big roots! And you can't just cut off the stuff that's above ground; you need to get at the root source so it doesn't grow back. This may take continued effort, so evaluate what the weeds are and remove them with intention and care.

If you can cultivate more of what matters by removing these sometimes-thorny weeds, it's worth stepping into the messy places in your garden and doing the hard work. That's how it felt when I took that first Sunday off of work several years ago. I thought working 24-7 would grow towering trees in my life, but instead I was cultivating kudzu. Did you know that one kudzu plant grows at a rate of sixty feet per season—one foot per day? You can't keep a little kudzu around or pretend it's not there. It spreads. And honestly, I think kudzu is pretty on the surface. But it has the potential to kill everything in its path. Removing the kudzu of working 24-7 was complicated, but I kept thinking about what would be able to grow if it were eliminated, and that hope kept me going.

Keep hope, friend. Do all things with great love, especially pulling the weeds. When it gets hard (it will), zero in on the positive possibilities. As you remove the weeds, you are making room in your life for what matters most.

Okay, let's get to work!

LOOK BELOW THE SURFACE

Weeds have two parts: what you see growing on the surface and the roots below the surface. Some weeds disguise themselves as pretty flowers. What's above the surface may look harmless—beautiful even—but what's below the surface threatens to kill everything in sight. Distractions are what we see on the surface; they are the things that grow in our lives because of something deeper going on under the surface. Distractions may include things such as excessive social media, TV, food, shopping, negative thoughts, chasing perfection, gossiping, comparison, worry, or other negative influences and temptations.

Distractions themselves typically aren't the root problem, though. We can get rid of what we see, but we have to get to the roots in order to permanently remove the weeds. As I learned from my fight with anorexia, the real battle is always bigger than what is on the surface. We have to figure out what's causing us to allow distractions into our lives in the first place.

How did those little intruders get there? Maybe you are on social media a lot because you fear dealing with your finances, or you are avoiding a challenging relationship or a pressing worry. Maybe you clean the house and organize more than necessary because you fear not being in control of something in your life. Maybe you reorganize your to-do list about a hundred times an hour, color-code it, and write each item in your best handwriting because deep down you fear not being able to accomplish it all—it's too overwhelming. Maybe you purchase things you don't need because you feel an emptiness—you need to feel loved, and you fear not being worthy of that love.

Whatever it is, it's okay. I've done all these things too. The simple act of being aware of your motivations can be the most powerful step you take toward lasting change. Acknowledge what's there and dig a little deeper.

What are your most common distractions? Why do you think you gravitate toward each distraction in your life? What is the root cause of each distraction? Some possibilities include fear, anxiety, a need to control, or the desire to escape from a reality you don't want to face.

Questioning your distractions—meeting them just as we meet our fears—might help you see why you are allowing them into your life at times and how to replace them with new, good seeds. This is urgent gardening work, friend. Don't take this lightly. Be tender with yourself but firm. There is boundless growth and freedom waiting for you when your distractions no longer own you. Distractions are enticing and lure us in when we don't want to surrender our fears, let go of control, and face reality. Distractions hold us back from lasting contentment and growth.

The most common weeds I've had in my own garden—the same ones shared by thousands of women like us—like to disguise themselves as flowers, and their root causes run deep. We'll look in detail at each of these three weeds:

- Connectivity—"I fear not knowing enough."
- Comparison—"I fear not being enough."
- Clutter—"I fear not having enough."

THE WEEDS OF CONNECTIVITY

Connectivity is something we are told is essential for success: "You *must* look at social media, e-mail, text messages, the

Internet, the news, *constantly*. If you don't, you won't be connected, you won't be informed, you won't grow, you won't be able to relate to people, you might miss something!"

So what do we do? We multitask so we can stay connected *and* answer e-mails *and* work on projects *and* try to have a life. We like to think that multitasking makes us productive, but how productive are we really being if our attention is constantly divided? Wherever your attention is focused is where your heart will follow. If your heart is constantly divided, how can what matters take root into rich soil? There is no such thing as multitasking—your attention is either in one place or the other. You don't do two things at once; you just switch between tasks rapidly.

Instead of multitasking, I offer you an alternative: single-tasking. Do one thing at a time. Do it well. Or just get it *done*. Done is better than perfect, and doing one thing well is better than doing a thousand mediocre things.

Are you multitasking or single-tasking? Check yourself and your motives: Are you chasing perfection or numbing something you don't want to feel?

When our attention is constantly divided in multitasking, we tend to get overwhelmed quickly. So we might search for an easy escape: our iPhones, the Internet, media that isn't really social. The average person spends three or more hours on social media a day. What about you? Are you spending hours a day on social media, but still feeling—and saying—that you don't have time to work out, call your mom, or sleep? I know. Been there.

It's easy to laugh it off because it's so common, and we love to commiserate in our distractions, whether indulgent food, shopping, TV, or comparing our lives with others' on social media.

But what's laughable about living in pixels rather than on purpose? In thinking that the Internet is our lifeline to the world, we risk missing the real opportunities to live on purpose around us. Social media itself isn't the problem—social media can be a powerful tool for God and for good when used well. More often than not, though, it's used as a distraction, not the tool it has the potential to be.

What do hours on social media make us feel anyway? Do you click off of Facebook feeling motivated to go and work heartily for the Lord?

There have been numerous times I have wanted to quit the Internet. I *could* feasibly quit the Internet, but . . .

1. the things that bother me about the Internet mirror those things that bother me in my own heart and would still be there, and
2. I'd lose many platforms God has given me to spread His good news.

So I wrote down a clear mission statement for my social media use so that when I do go online, I know *why*: to encourage other people to know God. When I find myself wanting to quit the Internet again or slipping back into using it as an escape, I go right back to that mission statement to check my motive and get back to giving. I'm certainly not perfect at this, but my social media usage has been more purposeful since I put this in place.

Love God, serve people—on social media and everywhere.

PULL THE CONNECTIVITY WEEDS

I often fast from social media for weeks at a time to get my focus back when I feel myself getting distracted. What you are feeding your mind is your choice, and the food you choose directly affects your ability to take action on what matters. Everything we read, watch, or take in seeps into our subconscious.

I have a few challenges for you that have revolutionized my life and the lives of many others.

1. This weekend, no social media. If you are wincing already, think hard about why you are so attached to it. This is an exercise in examining your heart, not following a rule. Fasting from things we may be attached to helps us to understand what's driving us to them. Take one weekend off of social media and see what happens. You won't die. In fact, you might actually get out of the house or get some rest or have a real conversation with someone or start the project you've been dreaming about or get your head out of your phone or computer and where it needs to be.

   For me, this was a really hard step at first. But after that first weekend without multitasking between my marriage and my iPhone, I never looked back. I haven't used social media on weekends for the last three years. When Ari is present, I want to love him on purpose with my full attention, and I also don't want Grace to grow up thinking that the Internet is more important than the relationships right in front of her. If this seems challenging, many people find it helpful to delete the apps from their phones. You can always add them back after the weekend without losing your account. I realize the irony here, but you can look at the hashtag #SocialMediaFreeWeekend and join the community of others who have been doing this with me. Put "Social Media Vacation" on your calendar for this weekend right now. Done? Awesome. Proceed.

2. If you have a social media account bookmarked in your toolbar, delete it. Don't make it easy for your attention to be conveniently divided. While you're at it, set yourself up for success and move the social media apps to the last page of your phone apps or put them in a folder labeled, "Be intentional."

3. Clear the clutter on your computer. If this is overwhelming, start small. Close all browser windows and all programs, make folders, and drag files into appropriate folders or trash them. The same goes for e-mail. E-mails are just a bunch of decisions waiting to be made. *Make decisions.*

4. Unsubscribe, unsubscribe, unsubscribe. You don't need every newsletter available. It's inbox clutter! How much of the e-mail that you complain about is actual e-mail you need to read? Gut it. Turn off e-mail notifications from social media too. I went from an average of three hundred e-mails a day to about twenty meaningful e-mails a day by clearing the clutter and setting boundaries.

5. Turn off all alerts that could divide your attention: the ding when you get a new e-mail, the notifications on your phone. Turn off *all* the dings. Because I have a business line, I keep my cell phone ringer off all day when I am working. My mom, Ari, and my best friends have my home number if they really need me. Think about

it: Do you really need an e-mail about every "like" and a text-message tweet distracting you from your real work or your kids? No.

6. Use social media and your times of connectivity on purpose. Write out a mission statement for how and why you will use them well. Post that mission statement to your computer or desk. If you find yourself mindlessly using social media again, check your motive and get back to living on purpose in *all* things.

THE WEEDS OF COMPARISON

I used to get very discouraged when I looked at other wedding magazines. I didn't have their budgets or their stylists or their prop houses. When reading other people's blogs, I would get depressed by comparing my writing, organizing, or business acumen to theirs. I would see happy couples, and though my marriage was improving greatly at the time, I resented all the mess my husband and I had to wade through. Other people were reading large portions of the Bible while I had a hard time reading two paragraphs of an e-mail without getting distracted. Other people were better, faster, smarter, and more successful, and their lives seemed perfect. *Ugh!*

I wanted to be like them. Well, until God shed some light on this for me—a giant million-watt spotlight. Comparison is coveting. And I can see why God felt that strongly about it and forbade it in the Ten Commandments. Comparison makes me ungrateful, which is ignoring God's gifts to me. When I want what everyone else has, I am blinded to the blessings right in front of me. When I give Grace a hug, she doesn't say, "Mama, this hug isn't as good as the one you gave Daddy!" She accepts it with joy. God delights in us doing the same.

Comparison isn't only the thief of joy; it's the thief of everything. If you are comparing your business, work, kids, marriage, finances, spiritual maturity, smarts, or _____[insert whatever it is for you] to those of any other human being on this earth, you will continue to chase your tail, and you will *miss your life.*

In what specific ways or areas have you been comparing yourself to others? What has comparison been stealing from your life?

I was so there. I chased "big" and "more, more, more" and "the best" and "more followers" and—you get the picture—for way too long. Until all those things I had worked so hard to build by comparing myself to others started to crumble.

Living on purpose turns comparison and coveting into compassion and cheering on. When you are living on purpose, it doesn't matter what someone else's journey looks like. All that matters is that you are going to the same place for eternity. You *want* to help other people get there. So why not be happy for people when they find success or joy or when something comes easier to them than it does to you? If God is glorified, the success is yours, too, my friend. We are all in this together.

This is why I believe there are no "industry secrets" or anything we have been given that wasn't meant to be a blessing for others. All that we have is God's in the first place: our money, our stuff, our talents, all of it. We are blessed to be a blessing.

Just because everyone is going in one direction doesn't

mean you should too. Follow the narrow path to make what matters happen.

PULL THE COMPARISON WEEDS

When you find yourself comparing your worth to others', get your head and heart in check and connect back to your purpose. Stop checking up on people in the name of *inspiration*. Connect back to what matters.

1. Make a list of three purpose-filled things you will do when you find yourself lost in the "I am not as good as _____" talk. Examples: read the Bible, pray, sing worship songs, use one of the creative gifts God has given you to serve others, or encourage someone in his or her faith.
2. Count your blessings and praise God for the gifts right in front of you. Every time you find yourself comparing your worth to others', drop and give me twenty! Twenty things you are grateful for, that is. This may take constant practice, but it will be worth it. Cultivate the new habit of gratitude for what you have over coveting what others have. A heart of gratitude turns what we have into enough—more than enough.
3. Pray. Prayer kicks me right out of comparison. The moment I start talking to God, I remember that we are all in this together, and He calls us to encourage and build one another up in faith. I remember my purpose. I remember we are all equals. I remember we are all His children. Prayer turns comparison into compassion and cheering on.

THE WEEDS OF CLUTTER

We live in a culture where excess is the norm. It's socially acceptable to have piles of stuff in our houses—clothes, books, toys—that never get used. Some would even say that having excess means you are more successful. Advertisements and media lure us in, making us believe their products' promises to make us beautiful, smart, stress-free, or satisfied. And then a newer version of that thing comes out, and we suddenly feel like that first thing is inadequate. This cycle keeps going until we finally see that the greatest things in life are not *things*. We cannot take our stuff to heaven with us.

After I gradually climbed out of my old life, my stuff was still stuck there. Cocktail dresses in my closet reminded me of late-night drinking at industry parties. Clothes with the tags still on them brought back memories of stress-induced shopping sprees. A stack of blank journals reminded me of failed attempts to slow down and reflect. I had so many decorative throw pillows on my couch that no one could sit on it. The act of digging in a drawer to find the spare set of car keys (since the main one was buried in another pile of stuff) just created another mess. My junk was multiplying junk.

One of my acting teachers used to tell us that discovering the heart of a person is like peeling an onion—you have to peel each layer to reveal the next. Our physical environment can be a mirror to our deepest layers, revealing chaos, control, or true contentment. As we peel back the layers of clutter, we learn just how attached we are to our things as a part of our worth. But as we challenge ourselves to let our stuff go *on purpose*, we find something deeper than the absence of clutter: the fullness of life.

I challenge you today to start clearing the clutter, not to make room for more but to make room for life—to make room for the invasion of simplicity that God has in store for you on this journey.

PULL THE CLUTTER WEEDS

For me, clearing the clutter was not a matter of tidying up and donating a few bags of clothes; it was much bigger than spring cleaning. I had yard sale after yard sale and gave dozens of bags of clothes away, but the clutter never seemed to end. I finally understood that clearing the physical clutter in my life not only requires letting things go, but it means not acquiring more.

So I stopped shopping. In September 2013, encouraged by my friend Nancy Ray, who had done the same, I decided to fast from buying clothing, home décor, and other things I didn't need. I planned to do the shopping fast until that Christmas, but as I type this to you months later, I'm still going. I've learned in this fast that God's comfort lasts far beyond a new outfit. I have a long way to go in aligning my heart with God's (it's still hard for me to walk through Target and not want to buy things I don't need!), but I'm grateful for what this fast has already taught me.

Simplify, and question everything. Look at your office, your closet, or your whole house, and ask yourself this question about each item you see: *Is this helping me live out God's purpose?* If the answer is no or you aren't sure, write the item down. At the top of your list write: *You can't take it to heaven with you!* Allow yourself to be challenged because it might simplify and open your life. Pray and ask God how He would like each item to be used.

Repeat after me: clutter out; purpose in. The Christmas cards from 2008, old magazines, former business cards, and even prized possessions that you know someone else could use more than you—let them go. Consider what good you could do for others and for your family. For everything you get rid of, you open your life to let purpose in.

Choose purpose over purchase.

CLEAR MENTAL CLUTTER

Then there is the stuff that swims in our noggins: the mental clutter.

What percentage of your purpose potential would you say you've been using lately? Many of us are operating at less than 10 percent because there's stuff in the way. Have you ever been in bed at night, unable to sleep because your wheels keep turning? Worries, fears, projects, and unsettled thoughts keep us awake—like the perpetual dirt cloud around Pigpen in the *Peanuts* comic strip. That stuff will follow you until you do something about it and clear the clutter. We have only a finite amount of mental space and energy every day.

How can we live on purpose if 90 percent of our brains are packed with junk? How can we realize our fullest potential when we are spending so much time seeking approval from others? How can you be present if your head is somewhere else?

If something in your head—or in your office or on your

desk or in your car or in your purse—doesn't fuel God's purpose for you, it's clutter, and it will swim in your head till you give it to Him.

But have no fear. There is a way out. It's so easy to begin to clear that clutter. The reasons we don't do it most of the time:

1. We declare that we can't because we don't have time, money, or energy. If you want to live on purpose, you will make time. You already are by reading this book. No matter your circumstances, you have enough time to make a change. And living on purpose doesn't cost money; it costs heart and pride, among many other things. Don't get overwhelmed by thinking you need an endless amount of energy to make a change; you need only the energy to take the first step. Then you can take the step after that.

2. We have a fear of success. We think things like, *What would happen if everything on my big to-do list were done? What would happen if I reached my potential and really lived on purpose? What would that call me to do? What would people expect of me? I'm not ready!* It's okay not to be ready. In fact, it's normal to feel that way because, perhaps, we *aren't* ready. The truth is that success doesn't typically happen overnight. Thankfully, true success takes time, and in that time God can prepare and equip us. A woman doesn't become pregnant one day then have a baby the next day. She has nine months to get things ready. For me, those nine months were heart-changing. I needed every hour He gave me to prepare for Grace. If God is calling you to something greater, He will equip you in His way and timing.

3. You don't know how or where to begin. The to-do list you

have on paper is overwhelming, but the Big List in your head is *paralyzing*. You don't even know where to start, so you don't do anything. You pretend it's not there, thinking, *If it's not on paper, it doesn't exist!* Denial about what's weighing you down, though, is usually worse than the things you are worrying about themselves. Denial leads to fear and stress about the unknown. It's self-sabotage, and it spins out of control till you take the reins.

Let's feel the fear and do something about the mental clutter together, shall we? If you want a form to guide you through these steps, check out the free printable at www.LaraCasey .com/makeithappen.

THREE STEPS TO CLEARING MENTAL CLUTTER

1. DOWNLOAD

Start small. Start by writing it all down—everything in your mind. I call this "downloading." If you are reading this book right now, you have enough time to do this exercise. Look at the clock and give yourself ten minutes to download all the thoughts in your head on paper. If you have time to check Facebook or Twitter today, you have ten minutes to create a big shift in your life by doing this. Right? *Right.* No excuses. Life is too short. Take a deep breath and start writing everything out—every to-do, project (big or small), worry, fear, prayer, everything! No stopping; just writing.

Take deep breaths and be honest with yourself as you let the words spill out on the paper for a full ten minutes. There are no rules to how you write; just get the stuff out. You can write in complete sentences, single words, bullet points, scribbles, whatever. Write honestly. And when you think you have nothing else to download, keep writing. Sometimes we stop because we get anxious or fearful about something we just wrote or something we don't want to write. Stay with it and get the clutter out of your head and on paper. As you practice downloading your thoughts every day, you will begin to understand your thought patterns and where you might need to go to God more.

2. CHOOSE THREE THINGS

When your ten minutes are up, look over what you wrote and pick three things (projects, worries, or tasks) to focus on. I suggest starting with the most overwhelming items on your download list. Chipping away at those will make you so fired up to do the rest! Just three things for now, okay? Control yourself, overachievers! Three things a day, every day this week. If you do more than that, awesome. Rewrite the three things—projects, worries, tasks—you are going to work on first with three action steps under each.

Making things happen is all about taking positive, purpose-filled action. Learning how to break things down into action steps is an essential skill. Action steps have to be

1. physical: thinking about something doesn't count;
2. small: accomplishable in less than a couple minutes; and
3. realistic: you have to be able to do them where you are with what you have.

If you are overwhelmed by an action step or know you likely

won't do it today, you probably didn't break it down enough. For example, "Reply to all my e-mails" is not an action step. "Sit down at my desk, put on some great music, open my computer, open my e-mail, and read the card on my desk that notes, 'E-mail is just a bunch of decisions that need to be made. Make decisions!'" Those are action steps. Those are physical, realistic, and small steps. Thinking about something doesn't count.

How many of the tasks on your general to-do list have been there for months (or years)? Things like "get teeth cleaned" or "get oil changed" can stay on our lists forever and nag at us every day that they are not checked off. In our minds we think that getting those not-so-fun tasks done will somehow take days when, in reality, they take just *moments* to set up and not very much time to accomplish.

To go to the dentist to get my teeth cleaned, my physical, small (under two minutes), realistic steps would be:

1. Open my computer and open Google.com.
2. Google the name of my dentist and find the dental office's phone number.
3. Pick up my phone, dial the number, and call while I open my calendar.

Making a dentist appointment takes me less than two minutes. Yet we put these "big tasks" off with excuses like, "I don't have time!" What we really don't have time for are the things that are taking up our mental space every day. Going to get my teeth cleaned—which took me only two hours, including driving time—and finally checking that off my list made me feel oddly free, as though I had a whole new realm of mental space on my list to fill with something better.

It has been the same feeling, *times 100*, that I've felt in working on things that are directly connected to how God wants me to live on purpose. While those action steps above may seem elementary, sometimes it takes us breaking things down to the smallest steps for us to take action on things, because we see how easy they can be. And many times—most times—the hardest part is taking the first steps.

You may not know what step twenty of your plan is going to be yet, but if you start by taking steps one through three, the next steps will become clearer. When I start working on a magazine issue, this is how it works every time: I get overwhelmed. Worry starts to spin: *There's just so much to do. How will I ever finish it all?* I procrastinate until I finally define small action steps and do them. Day by day, within a few months, we have a polished magazine packed with content we're all proud of. We make things happen when we make the choice to shift from denying of the unknown to starting. Even if we don't know what the final steps will be yet, they always present themselves.

3. DO YOUR ACTION STEPS

Do your three focal items with three two-minute-or-less action steps under each. That's a total of eighteen minutes max to start really making life happen. Some tasks might take fifty action steps to fully complete. Some might take two to fully complete. All that matters is that you start. When you finally do something about the stuff in your head, life is in motion, and there is no more room for fear or doubt or regret that you never took action. Little by little, action step by action step, the mental clutter gets cleared, and you have more room to nourish what matters.

I allow only three to five things to be on my to-do list each day, or I get completely overwhelmed. If I end up doing more than those three to five things, great. I used to keep my list of big tasks on my desk, and I felt defeated at the end of the day even if I crossed off ten things. Keep your daily lists small, realistic, and actionable.

Begin now. No matter how big or small the project or worry, you have to begin to make it happen. This isn't rocket science, but it will power up your purpose. And remember, the goal is progress, not perfection. Done is better than perfect. The quickest way to do something is to do it.

If you are stuck on what to do about your weeds, pray. Praying is an *action* step. Search the Bible for wisdom. You cannot go wrong there. I don't have all the answers for you, but God definitely does.

Besides the three Cs of connectivity, comparison, and clutter, what other weeds are growing in your garden? Name them and take action on removing them. Most importantly, follow God in this process.

STEP 3: SET
PURPOSEFUL GOALS

When you identify and remove weeds from your garden, you make room for new things to grow. You prepare for greatness by clearing the soil for the seeds God wants you to plant. That is step 3 of the process.

What is it that God wants you to make happen? What does He want you to grow to fulfill His purpose for you? What does He want you to cultivate to share with others? What seeds has He already given you that need watering? He may not reveal these answers to you right away, but He has given you some tools and wisdom to help you walk on His path and find clarity. He wants you to seek answers from Him.

Let's first look at the big picture:

- If you could envision your most purposeful year yet, what would it look like?

- When you envision your talents and resources aligning with God's purpose, what would that look and feel like?
- Why do you want to live on purpose?
- Where do you want to be when you're eighty?

I've asked these questions of thousands of women. The answers I've been given largely center on relationships. When we envision ourselves at eighty years old, having lived on purpose, we typically don't envision social media, comparison, or our stuff in the picture; we see people. We see hearts—hearts we hope to have affected in a purposeful way. We see those we have spent quality time with. We see grounded stillness. We see contentment. We see these same things reflected in the life Jesus lived—loving His Father and serving others. So the big question then is: If that's where God wants us, what is really important *today*?

Where do we start? We start where all life begins—with tiny seeds.

During the days of grief following my miscarriage, I ordered a copy of the *Southern Seed Exchange* catalog, a beautifully illustrated encyclopedia of Southern plant life. I needed something to look forward to, so I took some time to plan our spring garden. I read about varieties that did well together and would grow well in our zone, and I did some dreaming too. What would be good to share with neighbors? What would Grace love to watch grow? What would Ari enjoy? How could our garden be one of purpose?

There are two kinds of plants: perennials and annuals. Perennials grow for more than one year, and annuals live for only a single season or two. In the same way, there are two kinds of goals: long-term habits or lifestyle changes (deepening our relationship with God, becoming more patient, building a strong marriage, creating financial health) and short-term goals that have a specific end-date (running a marathon, going on a mission trip, completing a project for work). All our goals should be aimed at our purpose, but some need long-term focus, and some need to be focused on for only a season.

As we begin to explore living out our purpose through setting clear goals, pray about where God wants your attention in the long term and short term. How can you funnel every aspect of your life toward loving Him and loving others well? How can you use all the gifts and resources He has given you to live on purpose?

UNUSED SEEDS

There are some seeds God gave us long ago that are lying dormant. You know the ones I'm talking about. The gifts you think don't matter. The things you are afraid to water because they just might grow into something. The things you love to do but you feel like you're not the best or an expert, so you don't do them much or at all. Perhaps it's a gift of teaching or encouragement or creativity.

Friend, your gifts—the seeds of purpose God has given you—matter. Maybe those seeds won't grow into fruit-bearing plants that provide for your family, but they might make beautiful flowers that attract bees and make life beautiful, blooms that refresh the soul and can be given to others, spreading joy. And who knows, maybe those gifts *would* provide for your family— and a whole lot of other people—if you would just give them a sunny spot in your life and some basic nutrients.

What are those seeds that you already have but haven't sown for whatever reason? What are the things that light your soul on fire? Would you be living more on purpose—loving God and serving others—in doing them? If the answer is yes, what are you waiting for? Get to planting! If the answer is "maybe" or "I don't know," dig in a little more. You can always uproot a plant if it's not growing well in your garden, but you won't know until you try. You don't have to plant a whole field of it, just one seed. One tiny seed might change everything. You have talents and gifts that were meant to be used, not stored away.

I have a friend who loves to knit, but at first she didn't think it was important or worth her time. She even felt guilty when she would spend time knitting because it wasn't something she thought could help people or provide for her family. But God kept pulling her back to that yarn. When she connected her gift—this dormant seed—with God's purpose, a lightbulb went off. She now has a flourishing business and gives half of her profits to causes that have greatly benefitted from her contributions. Her knitting means something.

The things that fire you up in life can be a mirror to the way God wired your heart. If you are drawn to creativity, maybe He wants you to use those gifts to glorify Him. If you are drawn to teaching, perhaps that means something. If you are drawn to logistics and numbers, it's possible God has something for you there.

No matter your age or circumstances, if God wants you to use a gift for Him, He will make it happen. If you come alive in the kitchen, like my mama, maybe there is purpose potential there. Several years ago, at the age of sixty, my mom read an article in the local paper's food section about the Krispy Kreme burger: a hamburger patty, fried egg, and bacon sandwiched between two donuts. She took a leap of faith and wrote the paper to tell them she wanted to write a food column for them, centering on local, healthy ingredients. For three years she has been writing twice a month, educating thousands on the basics of wholesome cooking and Southern hospitality. She is living her purpose and helping hundreds of families eat well. And she is having the time of her life!

Write out what fires you up—the gifts God has given you and the places where you come alive, the things you love doing above all else. Set a timer for ten minutes and use the entire time to write about what fires you up. Push yourself to keep writing and adding to your list.

Now, do something about it. Use what you know now about breaking down action steps and take action. See how making the things on your list happen starts to shape your life and, most important, the lives of everyone around you. God gave us talents and gifts that are meant to be used to shine His glory brightly.

SET GOOD GOALS

With the big picture in mind and knowing some of the gifts God has given you that are waiting to be used, let's *make it happen.* Commit to the pursuit of *purpose* through setting clear goals and taking risks for what matters most. Know that this is a process— the idea isn't to have a perfect list of goals right away. Put your focus where God wants it, in His timing, not letting fear keep you from taking leaps of faith. Do what matters and forget the rest.

There are lots of ways to make money and find quick happiness. There are lots of ways to get really busy and then be totally burned out. But there is only one path to purpose: Jesus. He wants us to commit to slow cooking, instead of microwaving, our lives. Microwaving a batch of cinnamon rolls turns them into a hot, soggy mess; cooking them slowly in the oven gives you a dish of baked goodness to share. So set good goals—set God goals!

Read through all you have written so far in our Guide to Make It Happen adventure so you have it fresh in your mind. Pray about it. Ask God to guide you and show you where He wants your focus. Before you set any goals, commit your plans to God.

After praying and reviewing all you've written, be bold and write out possible goals. This doesn't need to be organized in any formal way at first; just get some ideas on paper. Remember, make a mess with that pen and paper! In growing new things, you have to be willing to get your hands dirty. This is garden *planning*, not *planting* yet.

- What seeds do I want to plant in my garden?
- What do I want to start in my life and why?
- What long-term goals would help me live on purpose?
- What short-term goals would help me live on purpose?

Check your possible goals to see if they truly are good goals. It's easy to make goals that sound good or goals that other people have that you think you should have, too, just to keep up. Don't do that. The idea here is for you to simplify your life, not to give yourself a new to-do list of things that sound good. Living on purpose cuts the fluff. Be specific and careful about what you decide to spend your time on. Every hour of your life holds the possibility to change someone else's for the better.

Do a goal check and ask these questions:

- Will this goal help build God's kingdom or mine?
- Does this goal also help other people?
- Why would I spend my time on this goal?
- Does this goal directly connect to God's heart?

If the answer to that last question is no, then it's not the best use of your precious time. Get into the Word. Pray. Change your goal if it doesn't align with God's heart. Focus on what really matters in the big picture. Will each of your goals matter when you're eighty? Or when you are standing before God at the end of your days? Don't run in circles with goals that don't directly connect to what matters most. See the big picture that God has for all of us, and write down goals that help fuel that purpose. Cross off goals that don't 100 percent fit. Revise goals that are not clear. Simplify, simplify, simplify.

Then—this is key—write down your *why* with every goal. Structure them like this: "I will _____ because _____." (For a "Purposeful Goals" printable to use through this section, go to www.LaraCasey.com /makeithappen.)

When I was a personal trainer, most clients would come to me with a number and say, "I want to lose ten pounds." I would ask them, "Why ten pounds?" Usually, when we got down to it, it was an arbitrary number, or what they needed to lose to reach the weight they were in college. There was no real heart connection to the goal of losing ten pounds.

But when we dug deeper into why they became out of shape

in the first place and what they wanted most in life, a picture of true fitness started to emerge. Instead of, "I want to lose ten pounds to get back to my college weight" (not very motivating), we worked on goals such as, "I will get healthy and strong so that I can live long enough to walk my daughter down the aisle. I want to live a long, healthy life so I can be a better husband and show my kids how to walk with the Lord." That works. *That* is motivating. Connect each goal to your core purpose, to something that matters to you. It will help you act on your goals instead of tossing them aside.

Your playing small does not serve the world. You never know how long you have left here on this earth to love others and change them for the better in that love. Taking bold action on what matters starts a powerful domino effect. The good you do today changes generations. Life is too short and too valuable to coast through, living by accident. Take your time writing down your goals, pray on them, talk them out with people you trust, and then *commit*.

I don't write about and study goal setting because I'm naturally good at it. I need accountability and some serious pants kicking to make things happen. Years ago I told my friend Natalie that I didn't set goals. She challenged me to set some goals that mattered. "Just try it," she urged. "God wants us to set goals that help Him shine!"

I lived for so long thinking that we should just sit back and let God make our lives happen. While there is deep truth to that, God calls us clearly in His Word to take action for Him and for the gospel. The Bible is an action book, not a casual read. Jesus had goals. He had a core purpose, and all His actions centered on fulfilling that purpose. While we are not Him, we are made in His image and called to walk with Him.

I want to model my life after the man who laid down His life for others and didn't care about material things and loved people passionately. I will never come close to having a heart like His here on this earth, but I think the pursuit of that will be worth all my failures and shortcomings. Setting goals is good. We need direction and a path to what matters. It's when we start setting goals that don't include Him or edge out His leading that things get a little—here comes my favorite Southern word!—cattywampus.

SAY NO TO WHAT HOLDS YOU BACK

Now it's time to set yourself up for success. You now know what worked over the last twelve months as well as what didn't work. You learned some very valuable lessons in all this. You are starting to see the bigger picture and commit to planting purposeful seeds. So what is *not* a part of God's purpose for you? Make a list of all the things that are holding you back (or could potentially hold you back) from making what matters happen. Write your list of what you are saying no to. Examples: social media at night, worrying about what others think, comparing my worth to others', waiting to mend relationships that need healing, making my phone more important than the people right in front of me.

Also write the fears you are saying no to. Fill in the blanks below:

I am saying no to being afraid of _____

because _____.

SAY YES TO WHAT MATTERS

What are you going to need to say yes to more often in order to live on purpose? In writing this list, you are making commitments and taking leaps of faith! But remember, when you are living on purpose, you have God on your side. "If God is for us, who can be against us?" (Rom. 8:31). There is great potential hiding in your fear of commitment.

Say yes to what matters. I encourage you to post your yes list publicly or share it with friends to help inspire others and to keep yourself accountable.

DEFINE ONE WORD

What one word really resonates with you for the coming year? Think hard about this. Pray on it. Then write that word in prominent places so you are reminded of your focus. Put it on a note in your car. Put it on a sticky note inside your fridge (I have one in mine!). Make it your computer wallpaper. Write it anywhere and everywhere to remind you of where you are going when you get off track. In saying yes to what matters and no to what doesn't, you are planting seeds. You are making decisions and setting new growth in motion.

PLANT SEEDS OF LEGACY

Plant things that will continue to grow long after you are gone. One of the greatest reminders of purpose I have is currently doing her farm puzzle at my feet. I told Grace I was writing things that I hope will help people. When Ari leaves for work in the morning, we tell her where he is going: to help people feel better. She loves knowing that is what he does. Ari and I work daily, amid our flaws and failures, to be a living example of the New Testament for her.

We know Grace understands, and telling her about the purpose behind our work makes us accountable. It makes both of us want to use all our time wisely and to the fullest to genuinely help others. I know she watches my every move and hears more than my words—she hears the heart behind them. She mirrors me all day long, showing me in human form how important it is for me to plant good seeds and live the way we want her to live. Now, this is also the thing that can paralyze me and make me completely lose confidence. Creating a living legacy for Grace in all I do is a lot of pressure, but it's a good pressure. Writing to you here in these pages, I am aware that she may read it someday too. That makes me want to write boldly and clearly, with tenderness. It makes me want to leave a legacy that leads her to the heart of what matters. It makes me want to plant good seeds in really good soil.

What seeds can you plant in others? What legacy can you pass on to those you love now? What can you teach to others? What traditions can you pass to them? What gifts of love can you sow?

Sometimes, the tiniest seeds produce the most amazing things. The mustard seed is one of the smallest seeds but grows into one of the largest trees.

Your seed might be starting a savings account for a child or grandchild. It might be teaching something that will help others—like volunteering for the Boys and Girls Club or teaching at your church or writing a blog post to share your knowledge about something. It might be writing a love letter to plant a seed of encouragement in someone else's life. It might be creating something—using your art and creative talents—to multiply love in the heart of another or to inspire many. It might be starting an e-mail account for your little one that you send love letters to daily and, when he or she is older, you give him or her the password to let your child read years of love. I have done that for the last two years, thanks to inspiration from my friend Jeremy Cowart who had done the same, and I love sending Grace special e-mails.

In the same way, my mom gave me the most special gift for Christmas. She gave me decades of family memories, holidays, and celebrations, her heart—her greatest passions and the unique gifts God gave her to share—in cookbook form. My mom is a trained French chef, and most of her happiest times have been in the kitchen and around the dinner table with us. She spent weeks putting together two giant binders of her recipes, kitchen tips, and favorite family memories for me. Now I can relive these memories with her in my own kitchen and pass them on to Grace. This is her living legacy.

Make a list of "seeds" you can plant now—perhaps in the next few weeks—of the living legacy you want to pass to others.

PLANT SOMETHING RADICAL

When I talk of doing something radical, I mean the kind of radical that changes everything for the better. That thing that has been set deep in your heart. That thing that scares you. That thing that feels impossible right now. That thing that you know would help you and everyone around you.

Radical literally means very new and different from what is traditional or ordinary. Do something different this year, something that feels bigger than you. Imagine the possibilities if you do! Maybe your radical is getting out of debt or starting a personal budget or getting healthy. Maybe it's finally going on that mission trip or writing that e-mail or starting that business. Maybe it's saying no to something or simply and profoundly choosing to be more still this year.

Before you get completely overwhelmed, remember to start small. You know the theme by now—start with a tiny seed. The core principle behind what I've taught at the Making Things Happen workshop is this: little by little, make what matters happen. Begin anywhere, but just be sure to *begin*.

Define your very first tiny, small, little, itty-bitty action step toward making that radical thing happen. If your radical is getting out of debt, your very first step might be as small as going to the local library and checking out a copy of Dave Ramsey's *Total Money Makeover*. Or get a copy from a friend. Or read my friend and coworker Emily Thomas's blog posts on personal finance at www.EmForMarvelous.com. Or sign up for a free Mint.com account to start an online budget.

If your radical is strengthening your marriage, maybe your first tiny action step might be writing a simple love note to your husband and leaving it in his car tonight so he sees it tomorrow on the way to work. Just an "I love you. I appreciate you." When you say "I love you" and mean it—even though he left dirty dishes in the sink again—that seemingly small step matters. When you forgive him—even though it hurts—it matters.

When you do small things with great love, it means something. When you choose to fight through the tears and still choose love, it changes everything. It changes generations.

Maybe your first step is simply to hug him. Nicole, our art director, told me that one hug increases your life span by three minutes, so hug it out more! Maybe your first step is simply to listen and genuinely ask, "How are you?" even if he doesn't ask the same in return. Maybe your first step is to pray for him. Remember, prayer is an action step—perhaps one of the very best ones.

If your radical is learning to be content and choosing purpose over purchase, maybe your first tiny step is to read my post on the Contentment Challenge (www.tinyurl.com /laracontentment).

If your radical is getting healthy, your very first action step might be to open a trash bag and step into your kitchen. If there is stuff in there that isn't helping you, donate it to the food pantry, recycle its container, or toss it. Imagine all the good stuff in your kitchen (and me) cheering you on!

I'm giving you these steps as examples—debt and finances, marriage, health—because *I once took these exact same steps myself.* The road to losing those fifty pounds I gained in college was hard. It was a long journey to learn to fill my soul and body with what it really needed. It didn't happen overnight or without struggle or failure or buckets of tears, but little by little by little, it did happen. It took me taking that first radical step toward cultivating what matters.

So what is your radical? Define it. Write it in black and white, and let it marinate in your heart.

My radical is _____.

Now then *do* something about it! Something very small. Sometimes—most of the time—the hardest part is *starting*. The rest of the pieces can come later. Define your radical now. Share it on www.LaraCasey.com/makeithappen, and let's support and pray for one another.

START TODAY

Plant good seeds. Start something that matters. Start today. I was going to wait until I was done writing this book to plant my new seeds. I thought, *I'm too busy—I can't stop to do anything else but write!* But the more I wrote, the more I kept thinking, *Why wait to plant new life?* Growing right next to me as I type this, in a sunny corner of my office, are about one hundred seedlings of various vegetables. What? You don't grow tomatoes in your office too? Every day I look over and am reminded that the best things in life come little by little. The tiniest seeds grew into these seedlings that will one day, with sun and nutrients, produce a bountiful harvest. God's design is beautiful and a perfect mirror to our lives.

Don't wait to start. Plant those good seeds of purpose now. You reap what you sow. Take the leap, break ground, and sow good things. A year from now, you could be reaping a bountiful harvest from a tiny seed.

Fill in this blank:

My life is too short to/not to _____.

Grandpa Cecil had a sign in his garden that read: *God lives in every garden. He loves each growing thing. Now forget your ills, get out and dig, and sing!*

STEP 4: TAKE ACTION

I used to come to the end of a year and get so frustrated looking back on things I could have accomplished if I would have tended to them little by little over time. I'd honestly forget about a lot of my goals. So I set out to change the way I approached them, doing the same thing God has taught me in gardening: nurturing. Step 4 is the most fruitful part of cultivating what matters—taking action through little-by-little progress (and maybe a few big bold leaps!).

DAILY TENDING

Breaking goals down into small steps—monthly steps, weekly steps, and daily habits—mirrors God's way of growing things little by little, with tender care and attention.

Nurturing a plant takes a commitment to gradual, daily care. You can't grow something by soaking it in a bucket of water all at once. In the same way, you can't work hard on a goal, giving it your all for one day out of your life, and then forget about it come January 2. Commit to daily tending. Our lives will bloom through daily decisions and habits—daily tending, nurturing, and pruning—not just the giant leaps made once in a while.

How we spend our time is how we spend our lives. The big leaps are important, but the way we live every moment—even the seemingly mundane parts of our days—can add up to a life of purpose. Remember: the enemy of taking action is the false belief in *someday*, so build your every day around making purpose happen, little by little.

How are you spending your days? How are the things you do each day helping you live out your purpose?

I used to wake up every morning, and before I even opened my eyes, I would reach over to grab my phone. With one eye barely cracked open, I'd start scrolling through e-mails, thinking, *I wonder what I missed since getting in bed at 3:00 a.m. I bet I missed so much. Ah! I missed three e-mails! And ten tweets! I should get up and go take care of all of these things immediately. No time for brushing teeth or exercising or breakfast; I am so behind!*

Does this sound familiar? I set myself up for failure from the moment I woke up. Before I even opened both eyes, my day was a disaster. I'd skip working out, skip breakfast, and walk into my office complaining. I was starting everyone else's day on a bad note too. And then I'd wonder why I never made progress on anything meaningful—I was just trying to survive.

Do you remember what it felt like back in school when you showed up to class unprepared? What about for that client meeting you just had? How often have you winged it lately? When was the last time you felt like you were running around like a wild chicken? Living by accident is no fun.

Living on purpose is a choice. Choosing purpose doesn't mean our days will be perfect; it means they will be meaningful, no matter what comes our way. Even when stressful situations arise, staying focused on the bigger picture allows us to transcend challenging circumstances and stay focused on cultivating what matters. The challenges do not defeat us but push us to dig deeper into our faith. If purposeful days are rare for you, then there is great opportunity for better days ahead, starting right now.

What helps you to stay focused on your faith each day? Make a list.

Remember, it's not about rules or being perfect or our own efforts; it's about living in response to grace.

Determine to make every day a great one. Do what you can with what you have out of a love for God, not to follow the perfect plan. Faith isn't about following a schedule or rules; it's about following Him—having a heart change and living that out each day. For me personally, here's how that looks most days and what helps me focus on what matters.

The difference between how I start my day now and how I used to is like is night and day, and it creates a positive domino effect on everything that follows. In saying no to my phone at night, I said yes to relationships and going to bed at a reasonable hour most days. This allowed me to start waking up refreshed.

I now read the Bible—even if for just a few minutes—and

spend quality time with Grace before work. I don't even look at social media until I've had face time with Grace and been filled with God's Word. Some days I don't look at social media at all!

When my work day starts, I usually pray before cracking open my laptop that God will use me and I will glorify Him in all I do. I have our company mission statement on my bulletin board so I am reminded of the purpose behind what we do. I know that every e-mail I get is an opportunity to live that purpose: loving God and serving others. I take lots of breaks throughout the day. I encourage my team to do the same. How many times do you go through a day and don't get up to eat or stretch your legs? How do you feel after a day like that?

Let's pause right now to do an experiment. If you are able to right now, stand up. Stretch for four seconds. That's it—just four seconds. Then sit back down. Okay, how do you feel? Even a four-second stretch break can make a huge difference in your energy and ability to think clearly. I take lots of good breaks for stretching, water, and Gracie hugs. These things make me more productive and clear-headed. I always have the Bible open on my desk, and my default browser window is Bible.com. It's so easy to get sidetracked during the day, so do whatever you can to stay focused. Our family Bible is always open on our kitchen counter, and scripture fills the walls of our home, my desk, and our fridge so we don't forget the big picture.

Why all these things? Because God brought us out of lives going nowhere, and it's easy to forget that when life starts moving too fast.

Write out how you currently spend an average day. How do you wake up? What do you eat? What do you feel in the mornings?

Where do you sit to work? What's your environment like? Do you listen to music? Write out a general description of how you do your days.

Now, envision living every aspect of your day *on purpose*. How could your daily life mirror how God wants you to live? Write out how your purposeful day might play out, from start to finish. Use all five senses: taste, touch, smell, hearing, and sight. Use what you have, in the current circumstances where you are. How can every aspect of your life be aimed at loving God—using all your gifts, talents, and resources to glorify Him—and serving others more fully? Even if you are in a day job that you don't love, how can you live on purpose in that job? If you are facing financial stress and challenges, how can you live on purpose with what you do have? No matter where you are, choose purpose. From the moment you wake up to the moment your head hits the pillow at night, what does your purposeful day look, feel, taste, smell, and sound like?

Next, envision living out the first five minutes of this purposeful day once. Just the first five minutes. How would that change your life? How would you feel?

Envision living out the first five minutes of this purposeful day every day for a week. How would that feel?

Envision living out the first half of this purposeful day every day for a week. What would happen? How would the garden of your life grow?

What if you lived your purposeful day every day for a whole month? It's almost unfathomable to think about, right? The positive possibilities are so big. But, here's the thing: it's possible. Start small. Start today. And remember: focus on purpose, not perfection. Perfect days do not exist, but making life happen on purpose is possible no matter what. It's not about having the perfect house, office, or stuff; it's about what you do with what you have. The people I see living on purpose the most tend to be those whose life circumstances are considered unfavorable by our culture. When the luxuries of the world are stripped away, what truly matters remains.

Rather than printing out a "purposeful day" schedule to follow, write out five essentials to focus on. The goal here is not to create a rigid schedule or a set of rules, or to live a self-indulgent day. The goal is to live on purpose and use what you have to make life happen for everyone around you.

What are the five core things that, if you did them daily, would help you to make progress on what matters? These are my five essentials:

1. Talking to God. My number one priority each day is to give my day to Him, committing to purpose, not perfection. If He wants my e-mail piling up in my inbox in favor of spending time with Grace, then that's what I do. If something comes up and a friend needs to pray with me about that big project I was going to tackle, I trust that God has a plan. I do whatever I can to use every minute of my day on purpose, but many times, those minutes get used in unexpected ways. Constantly talking to Him reminds me of the bigger picture.
2. Listening to God through His Word. Quality matters so much more than quantity. If you can get one single verse to live in your heart each day, that is something.
3. Exercising at least thirty minutes to stay healthy.
4. Nurturing my marriage.
5. Nurturing my munchkin.

Each of these things can be done in a short time. Besides physical exercise, none of these has a time limit. I'm not a failure if I don't read the Bible for an entire hour or if I don't pray for a specific amount of time. I can easily make each of these things happen daily. These are essential to keep the heart of my garden running.

Make your list of five essentials. If you want a printout to stir ideas, go to www.LaraCasey.com/makeithappen. Have your list out somewhere where you can see it often to remind you to take action on these things. Even if you get to the end of the day and realize you didn't have time to exercise, get down on the floor and do a few crunches. Isn't that better than nothing? The little by little adds up.

PREPARE ON PURPOSE

Living out purposeful days means preparing for them. Maybe preparing to live on purpose means buying an alarm clock so you aren't waking up to your phone every day, tempted to check social media. Maybe it means taking five minutes the night before to pick out your clothes. Maybe it means making your to-do list when you are calm and focused instead of hurried. Do you ever feel too frazzled in the morning to even make a to-do list? Don't set yourself up for failure by trying to make your list while your kids eat breakfast or on a hurried commute to work. Do it the night before. Set yourself up for success. When you wake up, you will know exactly what you need to do instead of flailing around trying to figure out what to focus on. Sound familiar? Is that you right now? You're not alone. That changes today.

Here's what I do to set myself up for success every day: I make sure I have enough healthy food for the next day for me and my family. I sleep in my workout clothes so I don't give myself any excuse not to get up and get moving the next morning. I literally point my gym shoes toward the door at night. I set a full glass of water by my bed for the next day. I make sure my office is somewhat clean. I pick out my clothes for the next day. How many times have you stood bleary-eyed, staring at your closet in the morning, hating everything in it? It's not because you don't like your clothes; it's because in the morning our brains are thinking about all the work that needs to be accomplished that day. Try picking out your clothes the night before and somehow that decision takes 1/1,000th of the time. Preparing the night before saves me so much time and brain space.

That entire prep list takes me five to ten minutes max to do the night before, and it saves me up to two hours of fumbling around trying to find things, clean up, or make decisions the next day. I go to bed excited and ready. Success is where preparation meets opportunity.

A reminder for those of us who tend to lean toward perfectionism: this is not about following a schedule or checking off a box. Only do these things—or whatever it is that will help you—if it allows you to be more intentional with your time. Do I do these things every day? I try to. But sometimes life happens, and God wants me to use my energy for something else.

Living on purpose takes making big changes—changes that may feel totally uncomfortable at first. But God doesn't call us to comfort; He calls us to Him. Set yourself up for success. Stop making excuses for why your day happened to you.

Grab a sheet of paper or your journal and write down three things you can do to set yourself up for success tomorrow: three actionable, realistic, tiny things. Do them. Prepare. If you do more, awesome. Don't overwhelm yourself though. Progress, not perfection.

Write down one thing you can do to prepare for greatness next week. Do it.

Write down one thing you can do to prepare for greatness next year. Seeing it happen could be closer than you think if you take the first step.

"A year from now, you may wish you had started today" (attributed to Karen Lamb). Start today.

PRUNING

Here are some more essential rules and helpful hints on your journey to make it happen.

As our gardens grow, we must prune in order to grow things wisely and well. God sets the example for us in how He prunes *us*. He prunes us to help us grow more fruit—lasting fruit. My entire life has been, and continues to be, full of intense pruning. Being pruned and disciplined isn't easy, by any means, but it's always fruitful. When God humbles me, I grow. When I fail, He builds my faith. When I try to do things my way, He prunes my heart so I get back on the path of purpose—*His* path.

When my friend e-mailed to tell me that my life was going nowhere fast and that God wanted my marriage with Ari to be put back together, I got so angry. But this friend was loving me as God loves me, pruning me for my good.

In the same way, with the same sacrificial, fearless love, we should nurture, tend, and prune what matters in the gardens of our lives. You reap what you refine.

Last summer my tomatoes got to be—no exaggeration, I have pictures to prove it—twelve feet tall! It was nuts. If you let even good things get overgrown, you are going to have problems. Those twelve-foot monsters stopped making fruit until I cut them back to a size that the nutrients in the soil could support. This is one of the best life and business pieces of advice I can offer you: too much of a good thing is too much. Selling hundreds of products from our shop sounds great, but only if we are prepared for that kind of growth. If we aren't—and we've been through many periods where we weren't—customer service falls through the cracks, and we lose our main focus: building meaningful relationships. Pruning our growth back to a healthy, manageable place makes for ripe delicious crops for all.

If you grow too many things in one small space, nutrients get spread thin and taken from other plants. I'll decode this tip in one word: burnout. You cannot be everything to everyone. If you try to grow too much and do too much, you aren't going to have enough energy to go around. I can't have weeks where I'm doing taxes, visiting potential preschools, trying to meet work deadlines, planning a large conference, writing a book, and preparing for a big church dinner all at once and do everything well. I have to either cut things out or delegate. Both of those things mean letting go of control, and God is all for that. Don't grow too much at once, or nothing will grow well. And if you get caught in a week like that (as I did recently), ask God to show you what to focus on. Prune your life in order to reap a good harvest.

Complete the task. Finishing the laundry means washing and drying clothes, folding or hanging them, and then putting them away in the closet. How many times have you deemed the laundry *done* after it's finished in the dryer? It's not really done until the task is completed and the laundry is put away.

In gardening we can't plant something halfway, water something partially, or prune just half the plant. We have to complete the task even when it is a hundred degrees in the shade, or things will die fast. Follow through in your tending, pruning, and nurturing. Follow through in taking action on your goals. Many times it's the last step—the last leg of the marathon—that is the hardest, but it produces the most results. Commit, follow through, complete the task. Do the hard work of pruning.

Refining your garden also means knowing when to pull plants out of the ground. If something is holding your garden back from flourishing, dig it out and start fresh. This applies in small and big ways for me. When we are doing an issue of the magazine, if a feature isn't working and I've tried every which way to make it fit in our mission, it's time to make a cut. The same goes with toxic people in our lives. God wants us to help *everyone* to know Him and do whatever we can to mend relationships, but sometimes there are people in our lives who can be like kudzu.

The plants in your garden shouldn't just fit for the sake of fitting or because it might be hard to remove them; they need to flourish and help everything else flourish too. The same goes for employees, projects, and the people with whom you surround yourself.

Evaluate often how your garden is doing. Focusing on your purpose and taking action on goals shouldn't be only a once-yearly event. You should constantly be aligning your life with God's Word to be sure they match and be pushing yourself to take big risks for Him. If you are only thinking about the big picture once a year, how far is that going to get you? Nothing measured; nothing managed. Watch your crops so you can pull new weeds that might pop up, fertilize when needed, give things extra water when they get parched, and prune what's growing outside of your purpose.

There is no substitute for doing the work of pruning. It's hard work, but it is worth it. In order to prune well, be present— willing to sweat and get your hands dirty.

STEP 5: ENCOURAGE OTHERS

The fifth and final step for you to create a life of purpose is giving. This is the ultimate blessing in a well-lived life of purpose.

Giving our money, time, resources, gifts, prayers, encouragement, and our whole hearts to others mirrors God's heart—it's why we were created. To love Him and serve others through that love is where the true riches of life are found.

We are blessed to be a blessing, not just with our money, but in *everything*. Reap the harvest, rejoice, and share it all—the fruit, the seeds, and the plants themselves. Our gardening wisdom was meant to be passed on too. Multiply new life with what you've been given, no matter how big or small.

Sharing the harvest nourishes others and encourages them to share what they've been given too. We have an abundance of ways we can nourish and encourage other people with what we've been given: blogging to inspire others and share knowledge, creating art, bringing meals to a family who just welcomed a new baby or is mourning a loss, supporting someone financially who needs it, using your architecture degree to help a low-income housing committee, teaching a group of younger women how to cook healthy food, baking for others, teaching a class, mentoring someone—the options are endless.

Every semester we have interns join our company as a way to further our mission and teach young students the value of marriage and integrity in business. We host people for dinner often, to share a meal and our faith. I try to blog as often as I can to give my knowledge away. What about you? What are ways you can share what you have and encourage others to grow?

Sharing the harvest shows those who may not know God who He is. When you give out of gratitude for all God has given you—not to get anything in return—you are loving your neighbor. This changes people. It makes them wonder where your giving is coming from.

Sharing the harvest builds relationships. When we host friends and neighbors for dinner, we are given the opportunity to grow in friendship and build one another's faith. Jesus spent a lot of time at the dinner table with people, breaking bread and building relationships. Sharing the harvest means sharing our lives.

Sharing the harvest creates an opportunity for celebration. Celebrating what God is doing in our lives is an opportunity to worship Him and rejoice. When you reap the harvest, remember where it came from. You worked hard, but it is God's light that makes things grow. All that we have, as I stated earlier, is His to begin with.

We can grow good things only because of His light. We

get so down on ourselves (my hand is raised high!) and get so overwhelmed by what *hasn't* happened in our lives many times. A surefire way to get you—and others—moving forward is to celebrate the good stuff. Giving thanks is one of the most powerful ways to refocus on the bigger picture in challenging times. Celebrate what you want to see more of.

Celebrate relationships. Plan a celebration meal with your spouse or a friend or a group of people you love. Ask your invited guest or guests to simply prepare to share what they are grateful for and what they are looking forward to ahead. Host the dinner in your home or go get pizza—it doesn't have to be fancy. All that matters is that you get together with another heart to celebrate the gifts of life. For some fun "Celebration Meal" printouts, go to www.LaraCasey.com/makeithappen.

GARDEN WITH PATIENCE AND PRAISE

All life starts with the tiniest seed—a seed that, with tender care, produces a harvest. Begin today. Little by little—and with bold leaps of faith—clear the weeds, plant good seeds, and tend to them with fierce devotion. There is a great harvest waiting for you at the end.

THE BEST IS YET TO COME

You know all those things you've always wanted to do? You should go do them.

I had just put Grace to bed, and Ari was already fast asleep. I was alone in the kitchen with a notebook full of blank pages—days ahead that had yet to be written. And I thought, *God, what do you want me to do with them? Whatever it is, yes!* Maybe it was the lingering smell of Grace's baby soft hair as I rocked her to sleep, or maybe it was the full moonlight glowing through the windows, reminding me of Grandpa's love for gazing at the moon. Or maybe it was God weaving together these senses and memories to bring the tip of my pen to touch the page.

"A note to self: you know all those things you've always wanted to do? You should go *do them*."

And so, I did.

I wrote down all the big scary things I felt God pulling me to, including writing a book to encourage others to make what matters happen.

Life is too short to wait to do the good things God has put on your heart.

The things that run deeper and are more thrilling than skydiving.

The things that God purposed for you long before you took your first breath.

The things that tug at your heart day and night, beckoning you to use your gifts.

The things that reflect His light.

If you see even a glimmer of one of those things, do it. Hush the hustle. Hush the chatter in your head telling you that you aren't enough. In God alone, you are.

In choosing purpose over perfect, the dreams God gives us may be hard because they are *bigger than us*. But, in Him, we are part of a whole, and we help others to know that they are too. We are never alone. We are enough. We are *free*.

Your purposeful path is waiting to be revealed step-by-step at the proper time—waiting for you to take the leap and say *yes*. And when you know *where* you are leaping, the *how* doesn't matter as much as the *why*.

Dear friend, the impossible is possible.

He can fill your empty places to overflowing.

He can set you on a path that never fails.

He can fill the garden of your life with abundant joy—and plenty to share.

He can give you new life.
The best is yet to come!

Surrender your fear. Take the leap. Make it happen.

NOTES

CHAPTER 8: TAKE A LEAP OF FAITH
1. Gary Chapman, *The Five Love Languages: How to Express Heartfelt Commitment to Your Mate* (Chicago: Northfield Publishing, 1992), 90.

CHAPTER 9: LEAP INTO WHAT MATTERS
1. Bob Goff, *Love Does: Discover a Secretly Incredible Life in an Ordinary World* (Nashville: Thomas Nelson, 2011), 25.

CHAPTER 10: FOLLOW THE REAL SUCCESS EQUATION
1. Alex Kendrick and Stephen Kendrick, *The Love Dare* (Nashville: B&H Publishing, 2008).

ABOUT THE AUTHOR

Lara Casey is a believer in the *impossible*, helping women to live on purpose through the many hats she wears in her parent company, Lara Casey Media. She currently is the publisher and editor-in-chief of *Southern Weddings* magazine, founder of the Making Things Happen movement, and a noted branding expert. Lara frequently speaks on business, faith, and how to make what matters happen. Lara loves to garden and explore local farms, and she wishes her neighborhood would let her have chickens. She lives in Chapel Hill, North Carolina, with her husband, Ari, and their bubbly daughter, Grace.

CONNECT WITH LARA

Website and blog: www.LaraCasey.com
Shop: www.LaraCaseyShop.com

Instagram: @LaraCasey

Twitter: @LaraCasey

Facebook: tinyurl.com/laraonfacebook

ABOUT *SOUTHERN WEDDINGS*

At *Southern Weddings*, we believe strong marriages, built on a firm foundation, have the potential to change the world. Come to our office one day, and you are bound to see one of us shedding tears while watching a wedding film submission or reading a couple's love story. Love and relationships fire us up.

We are not just making a wedding magazine. For us, helping couples plan a meaningful beginning to married life is like planting seeds. Weddings sprout the tiny seedlings of marriages. Marriages take root and grow strong families. And strong families, with all their ups and downs, have the potential to raise strong children—children who become wise and loving adults one day, adults with the potential to continue the domino effect of true love in their own families. This may sound impossible when we consider our own shortcomings, but it's not impossible when God is in control.

We believe that happily-ever-afters are built, not found. We want truly beautiful marriages—more beautiful than our weddings.

Read more about our mission at www.SweetTeaSociety.com, and join us daily at www.SouthernWeddings.com.

~~Should~~

~~would~~

~~could~~

Did